Siblings
and
The Children's
Story

KLAUS MANN

Siblings
and
The Children's Story

Translated from the German
with an Introduction by

Tania Alexander and Peter Eyre

Marion Boyars
London · New York

First published in Great Britain and the United States in 1992 by
Marion Boyars Publishers
24 Lacy Road, London SW15 1NL
237 East 39th Street, New York, NY 10016

Distributed in the United States by Rizzoli Int. Publ., New York

Distributed in Australia by Peribo Pty Ltd, Terrey Hills, NSW

Siblings originally published by Gustav Kiepenheuer Verlag, Berlin, 1930,
under the title *Geschwister*
© by edition Spangenberg, 1989
© this translation Tania Alexander and Peter Eyre, 1992
The Children's Story originally published by Verlag Heinrich
Ellermann KG, Munich under the title *Kindernovelle*
© by edition Spangenberg, 1989
© this translation Tania Alexander and Peter Eyre, 1992

Application for performance rights in the play *Siblings* in any medium or for
translation into any language should be addressed to Stefani Hunzinger Bühnen-
verlag GmbH, Am Zollstock 26, 6380 Bad Homberg, Germany. In the case of
performance rights in this English translation, separate application should also
be made to Curtis Brown Ltd,
162–168 Regent Street, London W1R 5TB.

The right of Tania Alexander and Peter Eyre to be identified as authors of this
work has been asserted by them in accordance with the Copyright, Designs and
Patents Act 1988.

British Library Cataloguing in Publication Data
Mann, Klaus, *1906–1949*
  Siblings and The Children's story
  I. Title
  833.912 [F]

Library of Congress Cataloging-in-Publication Data
Mann, Klaus, 1906–1949
  [Geschwister. English]
  Siblings; and, The Children's Story: a play and a novella/
Klaus Mann; introduction by Peter Eyre; translated from the
German by Tania Alexander and Peter Eyre.
  Translation of: Geschwister and Kindernovelle.
  I. Mann, Klaus, 1906–1949. Kindernovelle. English. 1992.
II. Title: Siblings. III. Title: The Children's Story.
PT2625.A435G413   1992
838′.91209--dc20   91–38140

ISBN 0-7145-2939-7   Cloth

Typeset in 11/13 Baskerville
by Ann Buchan (Typesetters), Shepperton, Middlesex.
Printed by Billing & Sons Ltd, Worcester

Contents

INTRODUCTION

In 1927 Klaus Mann and his beloved elder sister Erika travelled for the first time to the United States. It was an exciting time for them. Their father Thomas Mann was the most famous writer in Germany and a Nobel Prize winner, Klaus had already made his own reputation as a promising young writer (his first novel 'The Pious Dance' was published in 1926) and Erika was a well-known actress, who had entered into a disastrous marriage with Gustav Gründgens, the favourite actor of the Third Reich, later to be thinly disguised as the monstrous hero of *Mephisto* in Klaus Mann's novel.

Arriving in New York, the Mann siblings decided it would be fun to pretend to be twins, and soon they got written about in all the newspaper columns as 'The Literary Twins'. They loved the attention and happily stayed on in America for a while to enjoy their notoriety. When they returned to Germany they found the climate very changed. Klaus Mann had always been drawn to France and what seemed to him the more glamorous world of the French intelligentsia. He hero-worshipped André Gide and Jean Cocteau, admiring their liberalism and (secretly) their homosexuality. Cocteau's latest work, the enormously popular 'Les Enfants Terribles' (1929), appealed to Klaus and Erika, who understood only too well the make-believe world of Paul and Elisabeth.

In Klaus Mann's autobiography 'The Turning Point' he describes vividly the rich fantasy life he and Erika shared as children, when they played a variety of bizarre characters living in the shadow of The Magician (their father). In *The Children's Story*, his first important work written in 1925 at the age of 19, the children's games and secret language are drawn from his childhood memories of the family summers in Bad Tölz, Bavaria. *Siblings* was written in 1930 as a version of the Cocteau novel *Les Parents terribles*, but the brother and sister are now imbued with the characteristics of the Mann duo. The hermetic world of the play is a refuge from that world Mann abhorred, the world of Stalin and Hitler. Dargelos, the schoolboy crush of Paul, has also gone through a metamorphosis. There is a hint of the Hitler youth in the image of Mann's cruel daredevil described as blond and Scandinavian looking. A devil-may-care adventurer, hero-worshipped by the author, is a recurring figure in Klaus Mann's landscape. In *The Children's Story* he is embodied in Till, the attractive young admirer of the dead philosopher (another absent father figure) who enjoys a special rapport with the sensitive and pensive Heiner.

Jean Cocteau was irritated by the Manns; he disapproved of their meddling with his work and did not think the *Siblings* was true to his novel. He found the spirit of the play nearer to Thomas Mann's short story 'The Blood of the Walsungs' in which the young twins Siegmund and Sieglinde, exalted by a performance of Wagner's 'Die Walküre', where their namesakes fall in love, return to the family home and 'forget themselves in caresses'. The public was shocked by the decadent brother and sister in *Siblings*. The new age of the Nazi Puritan had no time for the moral tone of the play, and only much later, after the war, was it critically re-appraised. In 1933 the Mann family left Germany, all eventually to end up in America. Klaus Mann devoted himself to fighting the Nazi threat. In 1942, he managed to join the American army and took part in active service. In 1949, aged 43, he killed himself in Cannes, in the South of France..

Tania Alexander and Peter Eyre

The sun moves all around,
Sets all the stars a'dancing
If you stay still, unmoved,
Untuned, you'll stand apart. . .

Angelus Silesius

THE CHILDREN'S STORY

A NOVEL

I

Ever since the death of her husband, Christiane and her four children lived all the year round in the country in a small Bavarian market town not far from the mountains. Life ran smoothly in the cosy villa, with its red roof crowned by a weathercock which turned with the wind. A large garden surrounded the house. In front, the curved flower-beds and paths were well looked after, but further down the garden became wilder as you approached the large forest, separated only by a loosely knit wire fence.

In the middle of the forest a home for blind children had been built. All day long boys and girls with those white expressionless eyes could be seen walking up and down, or playing in the shadow of the trees, often in the care of their minders, but sometimes alone, skilfully tapping, attended by guide dogs.

If you left the garden in front of the house you found yourself in the grey main road which sloped gently downhill and brought you to the village. But you could also reach the village by walking across the fields along a footpath, winding your way over the uneven ground.

The four children are Renate, Heiner, Fridolin and Lieschen. Renate is nine, Heiner eight, Fridolin seven and Lieschen is five. Mama is thirty-one, and it was with the utmost difficulty that thirty-one white candles had been collected for her birthday cake.

When the children were in bed and she came to say goodnight to them, she sometimes looked so beautiful they felt an overwhelming love for her, something they would almost certainly have been ashamed of in broad daylight. If Mama were sitting in the girls' bedroom Heiner would call her so excitedly that she would be forced to extract herself gently from Renate and Lieschen to go and sit beside him. Heiner would kiss her hands not knowing how to cope with these tender feelings. Like a suitor wooing his beloved he would engulf her with terms of endearment. 'You are so beautiful,' he would repeat over and over again, 'a thousand times beautiful. . .' and when he had no more words left he would stroke her and invent new words of tenderness to worship her: 'You are so fluffy, so yummy, so. . .' until Mama laughed and managed to free herself.

But in the daytime things were not always such fun with Mama. Often, when she was tired, her eyes became troubled and she would lie on the veranda nursing a headache. Wearily she would tell the children to leave her alone when they bombarded her with all kinds of requests. 'Run along into the garden' she would say in a flat voice, 'it's the perfect place to let off steam. . .'

However, there were two horrid little obstacles to 'letting off steam'. First there was the tutor Burkhardt, a capable, good-humoured young man with dark hair who comes for two hours every day with a brown leather briefcase tucked under his arm to give lessons to Heiner and Renate. Burkhardt is not himself an object of their hate, but the subjects he has to teach are so boring. Equally tiresome are arithmetic and religious instruction — and the tutor has the habit of threatening the severest punishment if homework is not done properly. 'I will enrol you in the local school' he would threaten in a menacing way. 'Tomorrow at eight o'clock you will be sitting in my class, our private lessons will be over and you will be the general laughing-stock if you haven't done your work by the morning.' Heiner and Renate would look at each other, overcome by fear and anxiety. They knew quite well everybody would laugh at them. The village boys always laughed whenever the four children from the Big House, glowering defensively, went for a walk, dressed in brightly-coloured overalls, under the protection of their nursemaid with her knitting.

During the time that the tutor Burkhardt is occupied with the older children, the younger ones feel put out and their spirits crushed. Left to themselves they lack the imagination to continue with the more exciting games they were used to playing with the older ones. They sit forlorn, playing stupid dice games, or they watch Afra, their beloved cook, resolutely kneading her dough.

Constantine Bachman, the nursemaid, is of course an enemy — much worse and more dangerous than the tutor Burkhardt. While the tutor has power over them for just two hours a day, Mademoiselle Constantine's interfering presence has to be tolerated at all times. She is quite likely to suddenly emerge from the bushes, knitting in hand, with an expression of utter indifference on her rather puffy face. Her eyes fixed on her work, she knits away with irritating agility, giving the impression of being both bored and ready to take offence. She is surely the personification of an evil enemy, the constant adversary, always invoking principles as she stands there, her blond hair set in lifeless waves, wearing a faded, colourless cardigan and a blue skirt. 'What new mischief are you up to now?' she asks in a cool, contemptuous voice. Look at her now: she lifts her foot and gingerly prods something which is of great importance to the children as if she wanted to test its stability: it was a building made of sand — an entire city — a palace of the Caliph.

When Mademoiselle Constantine was in a good mood she could be relaxed and amusing; the children would then be grateful and laugh at every one of her jokes. At these rare moments she would more often than not talk about Düsseldorf, her home town; she uttered the name almost sensuously and with such precision as if it were the most wonderful word in the language, pronouncing the first letter 'D' with a kind of decadent softness. She would even launch into little family anecdotes and amusing stories about her mother and her married sister.

'Imagine', she would say cheerfully, 'I arrive home late at night, maybe having had a little more to drink than was good for me, to find my sister, the rascal, tucked up in my bed to surprise me. But one of her hands had somehow found its way onto my little night-table in her sleep. As I grope for the bedside light I find my sister's fingers. And do you know what I thought? I thought someone had prepared some tiny sausages for me so that I had something to munch when I arrived home tired in the evening. I was just about to go and fetch a little knife to cut them up for myself. Ha, ha, wouldn't Liesbeth have yelled if I had done that. Oh yes. . .' she laughed lustily, 'that's how it was in my Düsseldorf.'

Woe betide the children if some time later they chose the wrong moment to tease her about her sister's sausage fingers. She would be so offended she wouldn't speak to anyone for the entire morning. 'It's an insult to my entire family', was all she would say.

She was at her worst when she received a nasty letter

from her fiancé. Then it was no longer possible to get on with her. At the slightest provocation she would have a go at little Lieschen until she reduced her to bitter tears, and when she had brought her to this pitch, she would get excited and smack her, hissing angrily, 'Now you have something to howl about.'

It was not kind of Mama on such occasions to side with Mademoiselle Constantine. When the children came to complain to her she merely smiled and said Mademoiselle Constantine must have had her reasons. But she comforted Lieschen all the same.

At moments like these you could almost have hated Mama although you could never have admitted to such a feeling. 'She is unfair', the children whispered to each other rebelliously. Their beautiful mother, meanwhile, sat with her hands in her lap, her eyes sad and vacant, troubled because she sensed the unruly children were temporarily estranged from her.

The children loved Mama most of all in the summer when she went bathing with them. If you turned to the left off the path which took you through the field, and walked for a short distance in the direction of the town, you came to the Klammer-Weiher, black and boggy, between the sinister fir-trees. Even the trees in the forest were not as dark and ominous as the trees here, casting their shadows over the water. However, in its darkest part the river Weiher took on a gentler aspect where water-lilies, round like saucers, floated peacefully.

More than anything the children loved the smell in the wooden changing-hut. It had a familiar musty smell of old damp wood mixed with the steamy aroma of drying bathing-suits and bathrobes. The children sniffed and breathed it in although it seemed to them rather disgusting and even indecent.

Mama sat on the diving-board in a black bathing costume. Opposite, in the men's pool, all the men looked at her with curiosity, but she kept her eyes down. Her beautiful legs shone white in the sun; it was thrilling to see her raise her arms and then, as if in a trance, a strangely dead and tentative smile around her half-open mouth, watch her climb down the slippery wooden steps one by one, her arms still raised in the air, until the black, ice-cold water caressed her feet, and she bent forward shivering but happy, surrendering her whole body to these caresses.

The four children sat in a row on a beam that divided the pool for non-swimmers from the treacherous deep water. All four let their thin little legs dangle in the water, splashing each other and shouting till they could be heard right across the lake.

Renate was the only one who was confident enough to swim properly. Looking very serious she slowly let her body glide into the water, quite convinced she would go under if she were to forget only one of the movements she had learnt so laboriously. Determined, she counted, with bluish lips, one-two, one-two, and bravely carried on. But Heiner became defensive whenever anybody suggested that he do the same; he feigned shyness, but really was concerned for his life.

The nasty woman in charge of the bathing area stood at the edge of the lake and joked with the children. Red bathing-trunks drying on the line looked absurd as they swelled up in the wind. In the men's area the men stood in front of their changing-huts wrapped in bright-coloured bathing-robes, smoking cigars while they chatted to each other. Some of them were acting the fool, puffing and panting in the water, making more noise than was necessary, their chests covered with bushy tufts of black hair.

Mama swam out until she reached the water-lilies and

the rushes. She laughed and waved with one hand raised out of the water while she continued to steer with the other, frowning against the glare of the sun.

In summer they would go picking berries with Mama. In the middle of a clearing in the wood Mama would sit on a tree-stump, surrounded by thorn bushes, limp and overcome by the heat. The four children, bent and crouching, scurried up and down searching and picking as fast as they could. It was a matter of honour to be first to bring Mama a full tumbler. Then Mama would pour the contents into the basket which stood beside her. But the basket was large and a great number of full tumblers was required to fill it even half-way.

Again it was Renate who was the most competent and capable. With her legs badly scratched she climbed about energetically and did not mind squatting and stooping. Her dark hair hung untidily over her dusky boyish face; her slim figure looked more like a beggar boy's as she silently went about her work.

Heiner, on the other hand, preferred to sit somewhere in the sun, cheerfully humming to himself as he toyed with a blade of grass. If anyone scolded him for being lazy, he would at once become amiably repentant.

Fridolin was the only one of the children who was not really good-looking. He had a gnome-like face, oddly framed by smooth silky hair, a somewhat wry expression, rather too large a mouth and a protruding chest. Yet it was most probably he who was the motivating force behind all their enterprises. Although he was very much Heiner's equal, he was happy to take orders from him. When they were out picking berries he was the most zealous, in fact he went about it with almost disgusting intensity — quite different to Renate's matter-of-fact, glum efficiency.

Lieschen generally stayed close to Mama and watched with wide open eyes. She felt she was too small and too fragile to take part in the duties and activities of the older ones.

On the way home you had to take care not to stray into that part of the wood where the Home for the Blind was situated. For Mama became frightened and trembled if she suddenly came across one of the white-eyed children with their blank but happy faces, strolling in the company of the devoted nurse.

On these summer evenings Mama seemed to the children to be more beautiful than all the fairies and empresses put together. After dinner she would walk languidly in the garden which took on a greenish-golden light in the setting sun. She would look across at the hills to see if they seemed near or far and discussed what the weather might be like the next day. Set in the oval of her face, her eyes glistened like mother-of-pearl as they idly floated over the scene. Nor did her eyes rest on the children for long; lovingly they skirted over them, her expression soon becoming distant and almost frightened as if she were seeing strangers.

When the south-wind storms came, which the children adored, Mama was nearly always unwell. She lay in bed with cold compresses on her forehead while, or so it seemed to her, the hills were coming nearer to suffocate her as they suddenly appeared so green, right there in front of her window.

In the meantime the children ran jubilant around the garden, with outstretched arms, and hurled themselves into the warm gale-force winds. As they ran into the fields, holding hands, their hair streaming in the wind, they looked like a chain of drunken revellers intoxicated with joy.

Meanwhile Mama lay on the veranda, somehow frightened by her own strange children.

It was in winter that family life altered radically. Black ice-cold fir-trees peered out of the white snow-covered fields and the Klammer-Weiher lake was covered with a sheet of ice. Everybody had to stay indoors almost the whole day, and in the evenings they sat in front of the fire with their books. Mama wore a velvet dressing-gown and was always cold. Mademoiselle Constantine required layers of woollen shawls to keep her in good health. Luxi, the dog, was very old and decrepit. Now a deathly grey invalid, he had once been Papa's favourite. The cold season depressed him, and he sat grumpily in his corner. The only one to remain happy and resilient was the fat cook, Afra. The children would go sleigh-riding with her. Taking with them a large sledge, big enough to seat eight people, they walked past farmer Zwicker's house to the sleigh run. The run was very steep, made even more difficult by molehills, so it was seldom possible to reach the bottom without the sledge turning over several times. Afra shouted nervously in a mannish voice, while everyone rolled about on the snow. Mama, who had followed them anxiously, watched from the top of the hill believing that the end had come, while the entire Zwicker family stood in front of their house and made rude comments.

During the winter months the children would read novels about life at sea or the story of the Nibelungen, abridged for children. During meals they would then regale each other with quotations from their reading to the surprise and astonishment of their elders. 'I know', Heiner said to his older sister, 'that you have no butter for your bread, Mother B, but nor have I, nor by God have I.' That was a quotation from 'The Captain and his Shepherd'. But Fridolin recited dramatically '. . . then Hagen of Tronje wept the first tear of his life. He wept for Völker of Alcey who was master of the art of laughter.'

Later they would write down their own compositions. Heiner would sit at his desk for hours and was angry if interrupted, but later he would consent to read bloodthirsty ballads out loud:

A certain proud young man of Sunderbad
One Monday lost everything — all that he had.
So he bawled and he jabbered: he raised such a din —
It was dreadful to witness the plight he was in.
In the end he collapsed on a sofa, quite jaded,
Near an oak he had planted, by which he was shaded.

But suddenly came a great noise — to his cost
As the tree and the roof collapsed: all was quite lost.
Despite all his pride the young man was forlorn
And he cried, as he perished, 'Why, God, was I born?
To be crushed in my room here by You in disdain?'
So he parted in sorrow, in misery and pain.

Fridolin admired these poems and even Renate could find nothing to criticize in them. But to Mama all this seemed foreign and strange. She understood it as little as she had understood her dead husband. The children resembled him in so many ways. Each one of them had inherited some different side of him. But all of them had in common an inexhaustible and abundant power of imagination, combined with a certain strength and seriousness — both these characteristics came from him. Yet every now and then, unexpectedly, there was evidence of the gentler nature of their mother. The mixture of blood certainly was a wondrous thing.

Their father had died before Lieschen was born. His death mask, mounted on black velvet, hung above Christiane's bed. With its large nose, an unrelenting pinched mouth, and a severe yet dreamy expression, the mask dominated the widow's bedroom. Her husband had been a famous philosopher, but she knew none of his works. He had always emphatically forbidden her to read them. They were just too complicated for her to understand. In the gloomy study, his books were arranged in sombre rows on the shelves. They, and all the other objects in the room, continued to be revered by her after his death. His disturbing, radical writings were discussed all over Europe.

When she first met her husband he was a Catholic priest. Later he left the Church under a cloud. There had been a dreadful scandal. His disastrously subversive views had worried even the Pope whom he had attacked in a vicious pamphlet. In spite of everything he continued to the end of his days to go about in a black suit and starched collar, while his white rosary never left his writing desk. His will stipulated strict instructions that the rosary was to be placed inside his coffin. Ever since this catastrophic feud with the Church, the philosopher dedicated himself to Christiane, whose background was a mystery to everyone.

Who was Mama? That question certainly did not bother the children. They knew nothing about the existence of grandmothers or grandfathers. Only once had an uncle come unexpectedly on a visit. He was Mama's younger brother, an actor who worked in the big cities. Who would ever have dared to say an unkind word about Mama? A beautiful, mysterious lady, she led a very solitary life in the country, occupied only with the education of her children and reverent memories of her husband. The occasional visitors, regardless of how far they had travelled, would be turned away by Mademoiselle Constantine without ever getting a glimpse of Mama.

In winter Mama was even less active than usual. She would wander about the house, humming and smiling to herself, or she would sit for hours in her room reading the Holy Scriptures. Sometimes she would keep busy doing her crochet. She would sit by the window, hunched, pointlessly crocheting large gloomy bedcovers.

At times she would get up and go across to the children's bedrooms where all four children sat huddled together and listened to the hushed voice of Fridolin telling ghost stories about Princess Mu-Mu, who had a habit of giggling and roaming about at night. Then suddenly they would jump up and begin to argue about how high was it possible to count — surely no higher than a trillion? Excitedly they would all talk at once: 'It must be possible to go higher than that,' Renate would say indignantly. 'How could there be an end to it? I ask you. How could there be an end?' Then Heiner invented a new number, the highest number of all, the inexplicable number, 'Infinite-Pox', he called it solemnly, 'it comes after the trillion and will be there for ever. "Infinite-Pox" will always be there.'

Mama stood inside the door with her eyes wide with terror. What witches' coven had she entered? No doubt her husband's secret and forbidden books were full of such things.

The children continued to while away the long winter days amusing themselves with these guessing games. It was only in spring that their really important games would begin.

II

Nothing could have been more complicated, diverse and charming than the games they invented for themselves. In deadly earnest they spent the day in a world which was far more cosy and friendly than the tiresome world of Mademoiselle and their tutor Burkhardt. A whole new universe rose up around them as they sat together playing in a sandpit or by the pool or even further down the garden; although here things became rather less familiar as closeness to the white-eyed children began to make them feel a little uncomfortable.

Heiner was the most creative of them all. In a bright red embroidered jacket he hid in the grass, holding two carefully whittled sticks of identical length in his hand with his golden hair falling all over his beautiful face. His aim was to avoid disaster, to defend his empire against a threatened attack. Fridolin proves himself to be a good adjutant. His devotion seems slightly false and makes one suspect devilish motives behind his slavish desire to help. He has a scurrilous imagination, and he tends to sink to unusually coarse ideas. Heiner concentrates on princes, archbishops

25

and monarchs, Fridolin prefers executioners, madmen and witches. Claws emerge from every tree; there is danger everywhere: *the gnomes are afoot.* As these games reach truly giddy spheres, Heiner, unashamed, boasts that *he is God.* Fridolin announces he is *the demigod* with even more far-reaching and greater powers. And who is brave enough to decide which one of the two is the more important and who the more powerful?

There are many kingdoms to worry about for which they alone have the responsibility. But the children themselves are not really Kings in one of these states — they are equal, belong to no party but represent the highest authority — they have the last word. They are there to protect their most beloved country 'Ouse', the empire where most of the animals belong, and all those who are helpless — everybody with large appealing eyes: Herr Gunderling's fat cows who look around so mournfully and the old dog, Luxi; the babies, grubby and surprised to be on their own, sitting in the farmers' yards; also the overweight elephant out of a picture book. Luxi is King of Ouse-land. He carries his crown with veneration. It is true that he requires a little help when it comes to government, for difficulty in expressing oneself and slow decay are characteristic of the subjects of this nation.

'Klee-Klee' is the name of the kingdom of down-and-outs. The name alone brings to mind malicious laughter, shrill whistles, stone-throwing and cheeky primitive guile. 'Ouse' and 'Klee-Klee' are enemies. They always were from the very beginning and how could it be otherwise? Ever since prehistoric times they had fought each other in bloody battles.

Recently, however, a second enemy has become increasingly dangerous, more and more suspect every day. It is 'Wuffig', the evil, powerful republic which has Mademoiselle Constantine as president. The shop-girls are the ministers, piano teachers torture the population —— it is truly a woman's country, devoid of any passion, a cruel land. Did Mama in moments of unkindness not also have something to do with it? 'Wuffig', the land of the grown-ups, without making too much of it, is even nastier than 'Klee-Klee'.

'Wuffig' and 'Klee-Klee' have concluded an alliance, but what good can come out of that? Ouse-land is threatened, that is certain, and the children get together in great agitation. It was not so long ago that Ouse-land had been defeated, it could have almost been destroyed. Kuli, the fat little Elephant King, had been the casualty on that occasion: Herbert, the chief down-and-out, had stabbed him at a sumptuous royal banquet. Rebellion and revolution followed. This sort of thing must be avoided now.

Renate, looking even slimmer than a young boy, wears a tattered jacket. Her hair cut like a page boy but in wild disarray, she stands tense, leaning against the swing, longing for action. 'You are all dawdling. We must take action at once. We must give the "Klee-Klee" a good thrashing!' Heiner cowers in the sand, alarmed, and begins to play with the blades of grass. Smiling, he withdraws from the thought of all that energy. Fridolin is confused by all this and with an air of detachment suggests various executioners and witches who might be at his disposal. Lieschen on the other hand remains passive and listens sweetly with wide open eyes, a charming dignitary from 'Ouse-land'.

Renate frowns fiercely and makes a thrashing movement with a switch ready for battle. 'This time, they must be taught a lesson', she declares with the cruelty of an Amazon. Heiner, gently and thoughtfully, pats his shining locks and dare not meet the eyes of his sister who tries to instil him with courage. Nervously smiling to himself he looks down into the sand and announces sadly ' "Klee-Klee" is very powerful.'

Everything can be changed in a trice. Gone are the kingdoms which have been fighting each other, gone is danger and conspiracy. The house is transformed into a luxury liner and the garden is the deck. Everybody is very adult and sophisticated. The liner is on its way to Asia. The fields outside have become a sea of green waves. Everybody has grown-up names, everybody is rich and no one need want for anything. Fridolin has become Monsieur Coeur de Lion and is a millionaire. Heiner is to be addressed as Mr Stonewell and his income of course amounts to several millions. Everyone meets in small groups for a chat. Baroness Baudessin, previously called Renate, has taken on a sport-loving, American personality; Mademoiselle Lieschen von Hirselmann, her little companion, has to remain in the background — which secretly does not please her at all.

'Oh dear', complains Mr Stonewell, so blasé that he talks through his nose. 'We are offered so many distractions on this liner — three theatres and three concerts every night — how, I'm sure you'll agree, are we to cope with so much luxury?' The smart Baroness only likes charging across the deck at night on her black horse.

Even the otherwise useless and stiff-looking dolls are drawn into the elegant goings-on. Miss Littlemiss plays an important role. She is the prettiest of all in a pink dress and a blond wig. Mr Stonewell's son Bobbie is unfortunately very frivolous and has no clothes on. His father can be relied on to tell the story about his son often going to three shows and three concerts all on the same evening. This is so excessive that Baroness Baudessin recommends a good spanking.

Mademoiselle Constantine is the ship's matron who is

not very much liked, but what harm can she do? People can ignore her 'Wuffig' existence by making clever conversation.

Look, the liner is making a stop. It is the island Karo in the great ocean. Will it be possible to walk a little on land? And would it be out of order to invite the ship's matron to accompany them?

Seen from a different angle, it could be said the bad-tempered Mademoiselle Constantine has come to take the children for a walk. Together they go down the cobbled village street where the houses are decorated with old emblems. The saints on the façades of the houses look threatening in their fantastical robes, and seem to be working miracles with outstretched arms. In the street urchins are wandering about in gangs. But the four children walk on, wrapped up in their game, chatting excitedly among themselves and acting as if under a spell.

Mademoiselle Constantine natters with the ladies from the haberdashery and carries on with her knitting. The children stand together to one side in their brilliantly coloured mufflers — a splendid group.

Behind the mountains dark clouds appear. The children huddle together as if they were afraid of a storm which might suddenly break out. Are they perhaps afraid of the blessings the saints bestow on them with their pathetically outstretched arms? This extreme gesture of benediction seems more like a curse. In the meantime the urchins plot how best to annoy the children.

Lieschen looks around uncomprehending, pretty like an innocent little angel. Heiner smiles politely yet distantly. Gallantly he addresses Renate: 'A beautiful city, Karo, don't you agree, Baroness?' Renate looks away sulkily from under her dishevelled hair.

Fridolin says quietly, with a cowardly shifty look, as if he did not like to contradict Heiner, 'It seems to me only cannibals and dwarfs live here.'

After that everyone became silent.

III

The children were still out on their walk when Christiane was handed a visiting card by Afra, announcing that a young man had arrived asking to see her. Mama lowered her eyes with that same haughtiness she had shown when the men at the swimming pool stared at her. 'You know very well I receive no one' she replied firmly, putting the card aside. She sat, stubbornly looking downwards, her lips pursed, as if she were an Abbess who had been approached with some immoral request. She had not even bothered to read the full name on the visiting card, although she had fleetingly noticed his first name was Till.

The gentleman was being very insistent, said fat Afra in a state of confusion, it wouldn't be easy to turn him away. Madame Christiane seemed irritable and moody. She turned her face towards the window with a look of distaste. 'All right, show him in,' she muttered.

The young man was not too tall, but very slender. His clothes were a little too well-cut and a little too frayed. He wore a blue silk shirt and his shoes were in bad repair. His eyebrows were his most striking feature. They were surprisingly bushy and arched as though he were always raising them. This gave his eyes a childlike expression of amazement mixed with fear. These eyes, wide and extended, were of a bewildering, gloriously piercing blue.

Christiane remained seated at the window, stern and contemplative. 'Please tell me what you've come for', she asked quietly, and with a patronizing gesture indicated he should sit down.

The young man spoke politely and fast, never taking his childlike, anxious eyes away from Christiane. 'I have been a passionate admirer of your late husband for a long time,', he said eagerly. 'If I had not read his work I don't know what would have become of me, both from a spiritual and human point of view. You will, I am sure, understand, when I tell you I felt a keen and pressing desire to get to know the house where he spent the last years of his life, his library, perhaps some pictures of him, and above all to get to know you, my dear lady,' and he bowed his head gallantly with a boyish and flirtatious smile on his lips, 'as you were after all so very close to him.' He spoke without affectation, choosing his words carefully, perhaps a little too quickly, but with an odd childlike candidness which was slightly comic and at the same time touching.

'Are you a philosopher and a writer too?' asked Christiane, still maintaining a genteel distance, although her eyes now began to shine as they darted over his restless face, nervously grimacing as he spoke. Her smile, expectant yet restrained, expressed curiosity. The young man began to smile, flattered by her question. 'Well yes, it all depends how you look at it,' he said. 'I write all kinds of things — in fact, I do all kinds of things.'

A few minutes later they were walking through the house to see what there was to remind him of the dead master. They stood together in the half dark in his black study.

'Here everything is as it always was, exactly as he left it,' said Christiane in a hushed voice. 'All his many books, his large paperknife, his ink-stand. . .'

There were only two pictures in this room: hung above the writing desk a faded copy of an early Gothic painting of Christ on the cross giving his blessing, writhing in pain, and to the side a large photograph of Christiane as a bride, her veil thrown back off her face, with a blissfully expectant smile playing around her mouth. 'He certainly loved you very much,' said Till, looking admiringly at the photograph. 'In the end I believe I had become a kind of symbol for him,' replied his widow, sadly but proudly. She pronounced the word 'symbol' with hesitation as if she didn't quite know what it meant. Till looked straight into her face: she seemed so anxious in this room with the books and photographs. He also saw for the first time how incredibly beautiful she was. He remarked, not knowing what to say, 'By the way, I also have that picture of Christ. I knew how fond your husband was of it.'

They went to the upper floor where the death mask on black velvet hung above the large mahogany bed. In complete silence Till stared with those wide open, innocent eyes at the white face as if he must never forget the smallest detail to the end of his life.

'He looked like a priest right to the end,' Christiane said, shyly breaking the silence. Till spoke slowly, in a voice that sounded frightened. 'But at the end he believed in nothing any more. His only conviction was that all the values in our culture were dead and extinct, that a great catastrophe was imminent, the final clean-up, the Bolshevik flood.' 'He was a nihilist in his last years,' Christiane said flatly in a sad voice. Still following his own train of thought and not really listening to her, Till said: 'It was after reading his books that I became a Bolshevik.' 'So you're a Bolshevik?' The young man laughed. 'Yes, among other things.'

They stood next to each other in front of the death mask which looked down at them in silence, and continued their disconnected conversation. 'His purely Catholic books have remained his best work,' he said after a pause, smiling, a different kind of smile. 'They are the ones I love most.' Then in a matter-of-fact tone, he inquired: 'Was he still a priest when he met you?' With downcast eyes she answered penitently, 'I'm afraid it was because of me that he left the Holy Church. I have never been able to understand this. I am a devout Christian.' She heard the young man's cold and forlorn voice: 'I no longer believe in God.' She did not dare to look at him, but she knew how terribly sad his eyes had now become. At that moment for the first time she felt a kind of tenderness towards him.

Christiane invited him to stay for tea and soon they were seated opposite each other at the little round table on the veranda. Christiane looked at him and decided that he was not really at all good-looking, in fact almost ugly. His mouth was too large and his nose undistinguished. But his darkish blond hair casually parted in the middle fell attractively over his fine forehead and his strikingly beautiful eyes. As she looked at him again she decided after deliberation that his mouth was after all quite beautiful, as beautiful and childlike as his eyes.

The children returned from their walk, announced themselves and said they would like some cake. At first they resorted to the menacing grimaces they liked to make to frighten visitors. Renate scowled ominously. Fridolin, with an awkward little bow, was quick to ask, true to form, 'Are we interrupting?' which made the young stranger laugh heartily. Soon he was on good terms with the children. He never asked them questions in that rhetorical manner so common to most adults, which made you feel to reply was of so little interest that children would be reduced to giving short and offhand answers. He gave his full attention to them and talked to them as if they were equals. They were soon at their ease and Fridolin immediately began to explain to the stranger that he was in fact known as 'Mr Coeur de Lion' and was one of the wealthiest company directors on the Continent. With a touching and sweet note of good humour, Christiane entered into their conversation; little dimples appeared in her cheeks and her eyes shone like mother-of-pearl. She asked Till how long he would be able to stay and when he was expected back in town. It appeared there was no one expecting him back, except maybe his brother, but he was on the point of death and if he were to die a telegram would surely summon him. So he was dying? Christiane was disturbed and saddened by this. 'The poor man,' she said softly, 'he must still be quite young.' Till seemed unconcerned. 'It is very annoying' he said, 'I can never go far from the town where he is in hospital. For weeks now I have been in this situation, the end could come any day.' Christiane could not believe she had heard him correctly. His tone of voice made her shudder. 'Is your mother not near?' she asked hesitantly. His reply was harsh. 'No. Our parents are both dead. We have nobody, there is just my brother and myself.' She suddenly saw the same look in his eyes she had seen when he had spoken of his loss of faith.

Casually he told them he intended to stay a few more days; he was living in the Forest Inn, not far from Madame Christiane's villa. 'I intend to work here for a bit.' He seemed vague, staring into space. 'There's something I have to finish, a short novel. I write occasionally for money, yes, on the whole only for money. . .'. The word 'money' had a disturbing sound coming from his mouth as though he longed for it and hated it at the same time. 'I need a lot of money,' he said and his eyes darkened as they do in anger. 'I never have any. I never have any money, do you know what that means? It is awful, believe me, it is worse than scabies. Money is the principle of life itself: it declines in value, it's become disgusting, sick-making and it's only available to the worst kind of person — for me it's inaccessible — it's completely inaccessible. Money won't stay with me, you must try to understand, it escapes me, it does not like me, it clings to other people, it cannot stand me —'. Suddenly he stretched out his leg from under the table and showed the children his shabby shoes. 'I ought to have a new pair of shoes,' he gave a coarse and menacing laugh. 'Sometimes I earn good money' he boasted, still laughing, 'but I have many requirements, there is so much I have to buy.' The children continued to stare at his shoes which he flaunted unashamedly. He was sharp and had a cheeky air about him; his clothes had obviously once been quite elegant but now showed signs of wear at the edges and little holes had been carefully patched.

Till was soon cheerful again. He talked further about himself, quite frankly, and he talked a great deal. Christiane looked at him and smiled, while the children sat listening attentively, as if they were at the opera. 'I joined a youth club,' he told them, 'from the age of 16 to 18. I wore a green jacket and firmly believed that with a little decency all problems could be solved. It was certainly my happiest time.'

He spoke about the many places where he had lived. He talked of Paris and Berlin, Cairo and Madrid, about what happened to him in New York, or what happened in Tunis. When Christiane asked how old he was, he replied, 'Twenty-one,' and was surprised that she laughed. Every now and then he would bring the conversation back to the dead master of the house. He spoke quietly and reverentially. 'Did he have a sense of humour?' he asked subdued, somewhat distrustfully. 'Oh yes, I can just imagine, a rather sarcastic, sometimes extremely sarcastic sense of humour.' He wanted to know which one of the children resembled their father most and in what way. 'I imagine that Renate has his dark eyes and has also some of his pride, and that Fridolin has inherited his peculiar kind of mischievousness. While I'm sure Heiner resembles him in many ways, although he doesn't appear to look like him. Yet I think that he must be exactly like him.' He spoke quietly so the children would not hear him; he didn't even turn towards their Mama, but spoke tenderly and softly as if to himself.

In the middle of the conversation he looked at his watch and said that it was getting late and he should take his leave. He was polite and used conventionally appropriate words: 'It has been delightful, Madame Christiane. It has all been extremely interesting.' With a rather old-fashioned lady-like gesture she offered her hand for him to kiss and smiled saying she hoped they would meet again. His lips fleetingly moved over her outstretched hand, and he said he hoped so too but, raising his head, he looked dreamily away into the distance.

He had a very soft light grey felt hat which he pulled down over his forehead, a cigarette casually drooping from his mouth. He looked suspect, more like a city man who strolls around the streets frequenting cafés, hands in pockets, with a kind of sloppy, roguish grace. 'Goodnight, dear lady,' he said again and smiled looking beyond her while she smiled and tried to meet his eyes.

The children asked to accompany the young man to the Forest Inn. They walked beside him along the stretch of main road. It was getting dark. He didn't talk to them nor did he take his hands out of his pockets. He whistled a long, sad melody which seemed to ascend and then come down, fluttered high then low, became softer then louder; he let it flutter like a black, lonely bird which he had permitted to accompany him. Outside the hotel door he said goodbye to the children in a friendly, quiet manner, but turning towards Heiner he bent down and lightly stroked his hair.

The children walked back more or less in silence. When they arrived home Mama had already retired for the night. She had asked Mademoiselle Constantine to give them her love and say she was tired.

IV

Next morning the children insisted on visiting the young man at the Forest Inn. Mama tried to stop them, blushing, but the children had no idea why. 'That's not possible,' she said smiling nervously. But her smile was not for the children. Happy and confused she smiled to herself. Heiner was adamant on this occasion: he had never before had the chance to see a hotel room — he was stubborn and wilful and would not be put off. 'Well then, if there is no other way out,' Mama said standing in front of the mirror, 'we had better go.' Actually nobody had invited Mama to join the expedition. But the children were quite happy for her to come and they set off together. All the way to the little hotel Mama reproached herself and lamented. 'It's very wrong of you, children,' she complained in a hollow voice almost mechanically as if her thoughts were somewhere else, 'the young man will be terribly frightened.'

It was early in April, a windy spring day. To the side of the country lane and also in the fields dirty-brown snow still lay piled up in heaps. Everything was soaking wet, you had to wade through the mud, and the fields were crisscrossed with streams and rivulets. The trees seemed to be laughing as they shook off the snow. Mama too was laughing, a silvery agitated laugh because the wind was out to destroy her hair-do. Her hands were raised to protect her hair as she staggered along, laughing. The children joined in the laughter, all five of them in high spirits, and cheerfully they greeted the stout landlady of the Forest Inn. Then they rushed up the stairs where there was a strong smell of greasy hotel cooking. After knocking on the door of number 17, without waiting for any invitation to enter, they burst into the room.

Till ran towards them dressed in black pyjamas and barefoot; his face was dripping wet and he brandished his towel as if it were a flag. 'There you are,' he laughed because the children were laughing. 'I was just washing — don't let that worry you.' He ran back to the wash basin and as the children surrounded him he dipped his face deep into the water.

But where was Mama? Mama had stayed downstairs. Had she changed her mind in the middle of all this merriment? Was she cunningly hiding somewhere? Or had she run back home? How tiresome of her! The children called for her, Till, barefoot and dripping wet, rushed into the lobby with them. 'Mama, where are you?' called the children, and Till shouted too: 'Mama, where are you?' But she had gone off and vanished, no amount of calling was of any use. 'We'll manage without her,' Till laughed and they ran back to his room.

While the children rummaged among his things, he dressed. They had never seen such a muddle of newspapers, brochures and books. Next to the 'Berlin Illustrated' lay 'The Will to Power'; the New Testament was next to an American fashion journal. Buddhist sermons lay next to a thesis on sexual pathology; books on nature next to dubious

new Parisian novels, brochures on Russia were stuffed
between photographs, cubist drawings and dolls. The
children excitedly began to look through the journals,
shouted with horror or delight over reproductions of the
expressionists, and giggling drew each other's attention to
funny title pages and unusual names. Till joined them, half
dressed. He looked at the piles of books and journals and
laughed with the children: 'Yes, yes, I know, I'm a young
European intellectual,' he laughed openly and gaily.

No sooner was he dressed than he announced they
should go for a swim. The children were appalled at the
idea. That's not possible, they insisted, all talking at the
same time. Nobody thinks of bathing before May. Only the
other day there was ice on the Klammer-Weiher. 'You'll
get lockjaw or something. . .' prophesied Renate preco-
ciously; but Till said it would be quite all right and was
already on his way down the stairs. The old lady in charge
of the bathing was unaware of what was going on and quite
unprepared for this invasion. 'Young man, you will catch
the worst kind of diptheria, I'm telling you,' she screeched.
Renate fully supported her and Fridolin became angry and
sarcastic: 'By Mecca and Medina,' he swore like an Orien-
tal, 'by all means, do whatever you like.' Till couldn't stop
laughing. He used all his charm and persuasive power on
the old lady employing all sorts of fantastic words of
endearment. Even Renate was not able to restrain him.
Heiner was the only one who might have succeeded in
deterring him from his plan. He had become downcast and
very quiet: 'As long as it doesn't do you any harm. . .' he
said in a low voice.

In the end Till succeeded in wheedling a pair of red
bathing trunks out of the old lady and disappeared into the
changing hut. She continued to mumble to herself — never
had such a thing happened to her before, ' . . . and in

windy weather like this —'. But there he was already, springing onto the diving board. The diving board curved under his weight and laughing and shivering at the same time, he waved to the children as he dived into the water. He showed off by doing a somersault and for a moment his body glistened in the air, then there was a great splash, and Till had disappeared. The children were frightened — it was lockjaw — they knew it. Heiner said not a word, but his face was white and he shivered so his teeth chattered. Then, unexpectedly far away, Till's head appeared above water, and puffing out his cheeks he shouted and laughed and with powerful strokes swam back.

Who was that running across the field? It was Mama looking very angry. Mama was panting as she came towards them and could already be heard grumbling from a distance. 'It's quite outrageous,' she shouted, out of breath, 'really, it's outrageous!' She stopped short when she reached the children and ostentatiously put her arms protectively round Renate and Heiner. 'I'm sure he tried to force you to bathe with him!' she scolded in a voice out of control. 'It is dreadful of him — it's a really nasty trick.' However, the gesture she employed to protect the children was artificial and stiff; her eyes were not on the children, they were on the swimmer who was now making powerful strokes as he returned to the bank. 'He'll catch his death of cold,' Christiane said suddenly in a soft and anxious voice, and she took her hands away from the children's shoulders.

Till had now come out of the water. Dripping wet and naked, his hair dishevelled, he approached Christiane: 'I'm not here to look after you,' her voice trembled. 'I hardly know you — do what you like to yourself — but my children! I know for certain you tried to get my children to take part in this madness,' and again she made the same unconvincing, exaggerated gesture she had used when protecting her children.

Till stood directly in front of her. He laughed and said nothing. His body throbbed like that of a young stallion come to a standstill after a gallop. He gasped for breath and his captivating laugh was breathless like the laugh of a runner who has reached the line first. The red bathing trunks made him look naked and undressed as if he had nothing on at all. His childish, shameless laughter at his own nakedness made Christiane think she might faint. How was she to resist him? Why did the earth not open and engulf her? She tried to steady herself; everything went black before her eyes. The manageress rushed forward to assist her. The children looked nervously at their mother, her face now as white as chalk.

The less she understood him the more she loved him. She would sit for hours, as if in a trance, and think: Now I love him. Now I love him. Even though the thought had come to her a thousand, and even more than a thousand times, it was still such an overwhelmingly new and shocking realization. Now I love him.

In fact he was more of a friend to her children than to her. He got on with them splendidly and there was an almost alarming naturalness about the way they agreed with each other. Very quickly he had become familiar with the complicated network of their games, he understood everything and was soon 'Ouse Land's' staunch supporter and 'Klee-Klee's' dangerous enemy. He had weighty discussions with the millionaire Coeur de Lion, he behaved gallantly and playfully with Mademoiselle Lieschen Hirselmann and knew how to amuse the enterprising Baroness Baudessin with daring racy anecdotes. A quieter and more affectionate friendship linked him with Heiner. You would often see the two of them walking in the garden or Heiner would set off, small and alone, to visit Till in the Forest Inn.

Till would also take the children for long walks way beyond Zwicker's farm; they would stroll aimlessly through fields and woods, through forests as yet unknown to the children where the trees seemed alive, towering over them like giants.

During these walks he would recount to the children fairy tales which were more vivid and strange than any they might dream up themselves. 'It would have been much better to have lived a long time ago — a million years ago,' Till told the children. 'At that time there were no human beings, not even those ape-like people existed then, they appeared thousands of years later, when they already resembled us with their cunning and shrewd natures. At the very beginning, where now there is nothing but water, there was the Island Godwana — now we have the sea but that was once the island. There you would find the first creatures from whom we have evolved over millions of years. They had scales on their skin and huge beaks, wings and paws, enormous eyes which fixed on you with a stare no one could endure today. They were filled with hate, and if they ever had the misfortune to encounter each other a great murmur and rumbling shook the island. They were as large as mountains and I believe their eyes were of a piercing blue studded with golden lights. . . If one of these early, threatening creatures were to appear in Europe today, the whole continent would begin to weep, such was the spell of their eyes. This look was as touchingly innocent as it was terrifying.' Till finished his story and laughingly added: 'With one gulp one of these giant men then swallowed the whole of a weeping, contrite Europe. Yes, this is what these creatures were like: horrific, innocent and disgustingly greedy.' He stopped laughing, lowered his sad eyes, and stared at the grass.

That evening they decided to frighten Mama. They plundered the trunk where fancy dress clothes were stored, dressed up and painted their faces. As Mama entered her bedroom that evening, switched on the light and stood by the door lost in her thoughts and dreams, a screeching noise suddenly erupted from all corners of the room. Dressed in a flaming red hooded robe, Fridolin leapt out from under the bed while Heiner, half naked, with a golden crown on his head made of cardboard and wielding a sceptre, emerged triumphant from the wardrobe while Lieschen and Renate danced together in black masks. Christiane thought that she had lost her senses, no doubt she was being mocked by a hallucination, she stared into space trembling, without uttering a sound. The final straw came when the fire screen collapsed and behind it stood a gleaming Till. He was dressed in shining silver and, stretching out his glittering arms, bellowed warlike cries into the air. Christiane staggered and grew pale; it was only when the five of them formed a ring and triumphantly danced around her that she began to laugh. She laughed without restraint but she could just as well have cried.

She soon felt irritated by the children; she was offended by the secret understanding they always had with Till. She was jealous, yet dared not admit it to herself.

When she was alone with Till she was frightened by every word he said; the problems he concerned himself with were way beyond her. He talked a great deal about Soviet Russia and about America and he looked anxious as he spoke. 'Everybody today must decide in principle between one of these two.' He spoke with force but looked troubled — she didn't know what he meant. 'They are the two powers which really matter at the moment, and Europe is wedged in between them — what a dangerous situation. Poor old Europe in between!'

Sometimes he unexpectedly used big, radical words in a different context and that worried her even more. 'Our young people,' he said suddenly, 'have for too long thought of themselves as having problems and living in a state of uncertainty. In fact, we are perhaps the least concerned young generation that has ever been. We only talk about problems, but we don't believe in them. We believe only in life — and in death.'

Everything he told her about his past was completely foreign to her and terrible. He boasted how clever he was at stealing. 'Yes,' he said cheerfully, 'I soon mastered that. I flirt with the girl who is serving and while she flutters her eyelashes and laughs I just pinch what I like: little bottles of liqueurs, small English scones, bottles of lovely scent. . .' What was Christiane to say to that? Nor did she like the way he talked freely and with great assurance about sexual abnormality. He could not contain himself with laughter because she did not know what a transvestite was. He was often quite irritated when she called homosexual love 'abnormal' as compared with heterosexual love. He showed signs of being offended when she contradicted him. He said: 'Yes, you are of course considerably older than I am,' with a hard expression, and looked past her. Then she suffered in silence. She was indeed an ageing woman who desired a young man.

Every day she desired him more and more as she understood less and less of his restless talk. When he was playing with the children in the garden, she stood at the window watching only him. She loved his hair, his hands, his mouth, his eyes, even his eyebrows, his voice, his casual, excited way of talking, his lack of manners, his laughter, even his depressive moments, the restless and marked face.

How did he behave towards her? He had known how to ingratiate himself as the admirer of her husband, but although he lived nearby, she hardly knew him. Was he not a thoroughly unsuitable playmate for her children with his tendency to use the kind of bad language you might hear in the streets? Mademoiselle Constantine had been quick to warn her. 'Madame,' she had said, stern and indignant, 'your children's new companion . . .' He had never shown the slightest interest in Christiane; how she occupied herself did not concern him. He never spoke about her, he never bothered about what went on in her mind. He is cruel, she told herself, he must know how I feel: why doesn't he leave? He is a wicked, a truly wicked man.

Yet she knew deep in her heart that he was good. She told herself: he is undisciplined, a deeply flawed character, he respects neither order, nor law. But these words were stupid and untrue. He was a better person than she was, and she loved him more than her own life.

Sometimes she was tempted to ask him whether at least he was happy even though he made her suffer so much. She dared not put the question — he answered it for her. How was she to accept him, how explain the contradictions in him? She had believed that his exuberant love of life was genuine because he faced life wholeheartedly without restraint or reserve. Then quite suddenly a fear of life, a hatred against life, would take hold of him. They would be sitting peacefully together when he would suddenly say: 'It is a shame, you know, that we are alive. When there was a state of nothingness, things were good, quiet and peaceful: this nameless state circled around in its goodness. Then some sort of evil convulsion came into play — what devil started all this? Who was the devil who injected life into the state of nothingness? Why was he taking revenge? What are they atoning for, those condemned to life? It is an illness, a terrible curse;' and then suddenly in a childlike and plaintive tone: 'I want so much to die — I want so much to be dead — I'm so sick of. . .'

Her tenderness for him was stronger than her fear. At moments like these she felt she knew more about things than he did, even though he was so clever. Often she did not understand the words he used though she understood the lonely desperate look on his face.

Her greatest joy was to see him become calmer, alone at her side. In the evenings they walked together down the path going towards the river.

Then it was night. Lights shone about her. The river flowed past them and the lights were reflected in the water, dancing peacefully on the surface. Occasional sounds reached them from a neighbouring workshop, the banging of a hammer, the distant barking of a dog. The trees breathed in the wind. The whole countryside breathed in the night.

V

The growth of love and desire in Christiane did not change her or make her more restless; she did not suddenly become impulsive or passionate with blazing eyes. In fact, she moved around even more quietly than before, silently waiting. She was almost like an animal, though it was not clear what kind. Like a heavy contented animal she strolled peacefully down the garden paths. Sometimes she paused, lifted up her head, extended her arms and stretched her whole body with delight — because she loved him. She concentrated on his name with such intensity that she felt his physical presence fill the air, and this would remain with her like a luminous image.

When evening came, after she had spent the whole day alone, it seemed to her she had learned to love him even more in the course of the long day. In the morning her love had been weak, a mere flicker, now it had expanded, grown in depth, becoming stronger all the time.

She heardly knew her children any more. If she saw them playing somewhere in the garden, they seemed like strangers, ugly, officious, lanky creatures. The children sensed a change in her and avoided her anxiously. At mealtimes their eyes stared shyly but critically at this new face of their mother. Her mouth, half open, was unfamiliar to them; they were worried by this beatified, numb look. Mama's heavy vacantly smiling face, bent over her plate, her gentle sleepwalker movements with which her white rather too large hands used knife and fork, fascinated and also repelled them.

Christiane paid no attention to her four children. Now she was no longer a mother. Her whole body and soul were waiting to conceive the fifth child. Along with her desire for his body grew her need to pray, a need she felt at all times. Holding her rosary in her hand she sat for hours conversing with God. There was not a moment's doubt in her heart that in these days of longing and waiting she was closer than ever to the experience of His mercy and His majesty.

She kissed him on the terrace, giving the children scarcely enough time to retire to bed after supper. Till was sitting silently at the table, his chin resting on his hand. She felt the hour had come, she walked towards him and put her arms around him. She closed her eyes. Once more she was overcome by fear of meeting the look she could never understand. She knew if their eyes dared to meet he would still seem cold and guarded.

As she placed her lips on his mouth his lips were dry and unyielding — his mouth did not open. Trembling with anticipation she found only the sour taste of his mouth. At last he yielded and his tightly closed lips began to part. He closed his eyes and now she could feel his hands tighten around her body. She felt such happiness that she was afraid her tears would fall on to his mouth.

But at once she was rejected. With the whole force of his body he pushed her away and retreated backwards managing to clasp the railings with both hands. In his effort to flee his body had become so tense that for one moment it seemed to her as if he were again reaching out to her. He stood, a silhouette in the darkness of the garden — where he would have liked to escape into the night. But to her it was as if he was coming out of the night towards her.

Unafraid of humiliation she went towards him. She met his horrified, tortured glance calmly. Now close to him she said shyly, naïvely, but certain of herself, as though it could not be otherwise: 'Come with me now.'

She walked slowly up the stairs, head bowed, heavy, her arms by her side. He walked behind her as if something were forcing him to follow her, but he followed nervously. He too moved with his head bowed, but his teeth were clenched, while her parted lips were smiling.

She sat on the edge of the bed and carefully removed her clothes one by one. Photographs of the children looking very serious in leather frames stood on the night table. Above the bed hung the white death mask of her husband, with his strong nose, unrelenting mouth, and wide shining forehead.

The beloved one stood in the centre of the room. The clear night air poured through the open balcony door. In its bluish light he stood naked like he had been in the pool. He stretched and shivered, his body was so slim, you could see every rib. Around his knees his muscles trembled. His feet stiffly pressed together were frozen on the carpet.

She was in the bed, but could not look at him. She closed her eyes. A thought came to her, a thought so sweet that she did not dare contemplate it. Who was it who had sent him to her? Did she not recognize the angel who brought disquiet into her life — as if her name were Mary and she were waiting for the Immaculate Conception?

Slowly he approached the bed, looking only for warmth. She looked into his face. The expression in his eyes was still harsh, but around his half open mouth she discerned a softer smile. She took hold of both his hands. She couldn't tell if they were burning or quite cold. She only knew they were trembling.

At that moment a different emotion took possession of her; it had probably always been present, but now it was stronger and more conscious, it grew and held her more firmly and profoundly than any sensation of physical love.

Her heart was filled with compassion for his body, a compassion so acute that it threatened to break her heart: *because his body stood there in the night.* So these were his shoulders, these his thin, frozen arms hugging the front of his chest; these were the knees she had idolised, this his forehead on which his short damp hair fell: it almost made her weep. This was his body, the body he had been given, with it he had to live, endure the cold, feel desire, be happy — this was his body, inspired with life, the only thing he had to give; here it stood, naked in the night.

Nothing could be sadder in this wide, wide, sorrowful world than this. The despair that can be explained has its origin in the mind and is therefore of little significance. But this is a different kind of despair, a body-despair, indefinable and deep, beyond our small powers of comprehension.

The tenderness with which she caressed his body was filled with compassion. She sat up, squatting on the bed, her hands stroking his hips. 'Come to me,' she said, looking up at him — but he just shook his head.

Twice she asked him to come to her and forget his pride, to shop shivering and get warm. The third time he gave way and she pulled him gently down towards her.

He seemed more beautiful than anything as she covered him with the blankets, wrapping him up right up to his neck. 'Are you comfortable?' she asked repeatedly. 'You're not cold now?'

He turned his face towards her; his ardent look gave the impression of someone who had waited for this moment for years.

Much later, after he had already long been asleep at her side, she still lay awake. Resting her head on her arm she caressed him — but this time only with her eyes. With the exactness of someone drunk with love she recalled every little detail of his body.

She felt she had made a small discovery — a little thought came to her which seemed beautiful and worth treasuring. 'There are two kinds of life,' she reflected carefully: 'the restful and the active life. There are two kinds of longing: one drives you forward, the other holds you back. When these two opposing elements marry, conception takes place.'

She smiled happily thinking she had had a clever idea — she who had always thought herself stupid. Happy and smiling she sank into her pillows.

She suddenly remembered the many nights of lovemaking with her husband. She saw again the large face which had almost frightened her, the dark piercing eyes, the huge nose, the bitter mouth praising her beauty with the exactness of the devout. During those unbearably long nights, the intimidating power of his mind had assumed control over her inert and peaceful body.

Now, she again bent over the sleeping face of this stranger she adored.

Which of them had she known less well? She shivered alone at his side on this cold morning.

Above her the mask of her husband, with his severe but serene smile, was also dreaming into the early hours of the morning his deadly earnest dreams.

VI

Christiane was still sitting in front of the mirror, her hair loose across her shoulders, when Till arrived. He was wearing a grey striped coat and a blue silk scarf around his neck; in his hand he was carrying a buff-coloured leather suitcase. 'I have only come to say good-bye' he said and stopped by the door. She did not even turn round, she merely stared at his reflection in the mirror while he stood by the door holding his suitcase. She spoke in a flat voice: 'Why? Have you had news of your brother?' He replied simply: 'No. But it is necessary for me to leave.' Christiane did not move, she did not scream, nor was she able to cry. After a long, long pause during which she had been sitting motionless as a stone, she asked quietly: 'Can I not come too?' In her mind she could see him smile. She saw his lively face above the bright blue scarf: his wide open forlorn eyes, his dark arched eyebrows slightly raised which made the furrows on his forehead show, while around his mouth appeared that sad, helpless, anxious and friendly smile.

She could see in the mirror he was coming towards her, and then he was there, standing behind her chair: would he bend down and kiss her? But he only stroked her long beautiful hair which she had let down over her shoulders. Gently and tenderly he let it slide through his fingers. She turned around and looked him straight in the face. 'I shall never understand why you are doing this.' She spoke without expression, against her better judgement, quietly, knowing she was deceiving herself. He did not answer her and already his wild mysterious eyes gazed beyond her. 'Yes, I must be off,' he said as he let her hair slip out of his hand.

He went into the class-room to say goodbye to the children, who were doing their homework with the tutor Burkhardt. All four children stood before him in a row. It took a long time for them to understand that he was leaving them, and when they did their eyes filled with tears. 'We shall meet again,' he consoled his young friends. 'Very soon you will grow up and we can meet in the big cities.' They agreed and looked forward to such a prospect. He shook hands with them all. When he came to Heiner he bent down and kissed him on the forehead. Heiner smiled happily even though he was still fighting back his tears. His mouth quivered, his eyes lit up with pleasure even though large tears were already running down his cheeks.

In order to accompany Till to the station, Mama had put on her grey travelling clothes, which she wore very rarely. They were elegant, but not very modern, the skirt was baggy, made of soft, fine material. Her grey peaked hat was most unusual. All the colour had gone out of Christiane's face; it was white and transparent as if it were made of some rare and choice material while her dark eyes, peering out under her white forehead, had a haunted look about them.

They walked slowly along the road in complete silence. Till had a suitcase to carry. They didn't have far to go — as they turned off the main road they could already see the dingy little station. Then came the waiting on the platform until the train drew in, although it wouldn't be many minutes before it came. What more could they have to say to each other? There was nothing more to say, not another word. They knew everything and yet they knew so terribly little about each other that it would have been pointless to begin to use words. Words were inadequate and wretched.

Peasant women had crowded around, women carrying baskets of eggs, and even live calves were to be loaded on the train. Station officials were being officious, people began to quarrel. A stout gentleman got excited and became threatening. Christiane couldn't wait for the train to arrive, she was counting the seconds — at the same time she trembled with fear when she thought it had to come, she could not believe that it would: there had to be a miracle, yes, the train would derail, several people would be killed — *HE* would be prevented from travelling, it had been made impossible for him to leave, corpses were in the way, he had to stay, he will stay. . .

But the train arrived; it drew into the station whistling and blowing. The stinking black smoke filled the little station. The guard shouted over and over again: 'Two minutes only.' Grey, cynical faces appeared at the windows of the carriages and made fun of the little station.

Till bent over Christiane's hand, fleetingly as he had at their first meeting on the veranda. He straightened himself and again looked past her into the distance. He dashed towards the train, he had to hurry and in a moment his face appeared at the window next to that of a stranger.

As the train started to pull out, Christiane shouted, and ran alongside the moving train: 'Can't I come with you? I've put my travelling dress on . . .', and with a look of despair she pointed to her old-fashioned clothes. She had picked a dress which she had in the past only worn on journeys, her travelling dress, old, but hardly ever used, so she would have been ready had he asked her to come with him. Now she had also given away this secret. Had he answered her? His last words were drowned by the noise of the train as it disappeared. With a final glance, dark and concentrated, she once again enveloped his face for the last time, before it slipped away.

The train vanished round the corner and the little station was empty again. How could she bring herself to move? How could she manage to get home now? She reached home without really knowing how. Had she stumbled along the road? Had the children in the street jeered at her, and the peasant women pointed their finger at her? How had she got past her own children, waiting for her in the garden, and what had she said to them? — Now she was in her room. Quietly she closed the shutters. All she wanted was no light, to see nothing, not to move — just to sit in the dark.

She prayed for tears as an act of mercy, but they would not come. She sat in her room in the dark and let the hours go by: she might have been a large doll sitting in the middle of the room. Nobody had the courage to come in to her, nobody opened her door. Time passed without her noticing. Then her pain took over from time, and became stronger than time. Pain was stronger than anything else, pain dominated everything. She sat and suffered; suffering took over her life, every breath meant suffering. 'When there was nothingness then things were good and quiet and peaceful,' she thought. 'This nameless state perpetuated itself in its goodness. Then something happens and fits of unhappiness return. Tears fall into nothingness; God wept in his loneliness. Nothingness received the dreams of God as woman receives the semen of man, and thus life is created. All life is despairing, all life is truly without solace.

What curse must they atone for, those who are condemned to live?' — She did not move, she was not hungry, she sat and suffered.

The day passed. In the middle of the night she got up from the chair, walked to the window and opened the shutters. She leaned out into the warm night, and was met by a soothing darkness she found invigorating after the oppressive, sultry air of her room. She felt a sudden release, stretched out her hands into the night, as if they could find comfort in the darkness; the wind touched her face and she at last began to cry. For the first time she whispered his name, whispering it into the night through her tears.

She went back to her chair, she sat down still crying and soon she fell asleep.

She dreamed about Till, a short but wonderful dream — she saw him running up a hill, he found it difficult and was panting, but he ran fast. He looked like a labourer who has hit hard times; greyish, torn clothes were hanging on him, and here and there his thin brown body was uncovered. He had a silver helmet on his head, a large, glittering soldier's helmet which almost covered his eyes. He was barefoot and his feet were covered with blood as he ran over thistles and stones. And who were the little figures following him? They were Renate and Heiner, Fridolin and Lieschen, all dressed in the same disguise they had been wearing the other day when they had so frightened their mother. The hill was steep. What could be the goal beckoning them up there? More and more children joined the procession, naked children, children dressed in rags. Till, their leader, did not turn round to see if the others were following. He ran ahead, his feet scratched and bleeding and his helmet glittering. Behind him the children jostled each other, naked boys with dishevelled hair, little girls in colourful outfits; there seemed to be thousands of children, thousands of thin little bodies running and screaming — Christiane was anxious to see what the destination would be to which Till was leading them. She couldn't make it out, it was hidden from her. All she could hear was panting and shouts of jubilation and joy from the children as they got near the top. Till stopped short, turned round and stood facing the crowd of shouting children. He pulled off his helmet and looked beyond them into the distance. He was their Lord, with shining eyes measuring the number of his followers. Then he turned and continued to run up the hill.

Days and weeks went by. Christiane began going for walks with the children again, and taking an interest in planning meals with Afra. You couldn't help noticing the strange and absent-minded expression she now had, the slow way she walked, or looked up, with a distant and indulgent smile.

It was a hot summer, hotter than ever before. The dusty roads were glowing with heat, the earth was grey and beginning to crack. The trees were longing to be refreshed as they stood withering and sad in the blue haze of the past weeks. The garden was quiet, only the occasional sound of people swimming in the Klammer-Weiher could be heard. The children had gone to swim. Christiane sat alone in the heat.

She knew already she was pregnant. She felt no happiness, nor was she capable any longer of feeling new sorrow. She accepted it in a kind of daze almost as if she did not understand it.

Summer was all around her, the air was blue and vibrating. Beetles crawled slowly over the grass, sunflowers wearily held up their heavy heads. Outside a little old peasant could be seen slowly walking past. 'Let another child be born into the world,' Christiane thought gloomily, 'it won't make any difference. It just means one more person will have to bear the burdens of this earth. . .'.

Perhaps her brother would arrive soon. She had written to say that she needed him.

VII

Before the children had time to object, Mama's brother Gaston arrived. She seemed to have been expecting him for some time but had never mentioned it. When she greeted him at the station she grew pale with happiness. 'Here you are at last,' she said with a deep sigh as if someone had come whom, day after day, she had yearned for.

The children looked shyly and nervously at the young uncle they hardly knew. They thought him more handsome than any other person they had ever seen. In his own way he was much, much more beautiful than Mama. The colouring of his face was very different to that of ordinary people, above all around the eyes, and his mouth with its serious expression and dark red lips had a surprising, almost painful beauty.

He bent over Mama's hand and only said a few words, but he kissed her hand with deep respect and intense seriousness. Towards the children he was at first very reserved. Although he smiled at them his smile seemed to them even more intimidating than his impassive face.

They went together along the path across the fields, ignoring the damp cold evening air. Mama walked arm in arm with her brother without saying anything. Gaston was wearing a dark loose-fitting coat with upturned collar. He had pulled his hat right down over his face. His step was unusually springy, not exactly graceful, even quite heavy, but he walked with energy. He had broken off a long branch and with this in his hand he looked as if he had come down from the hills, where in solitude he had been watching over the goats and conversing with the white cows.

The children speculated secretly among themselves as to what his age might be. Heiner was certain that he was younger than Mama, no more than twenty. But Renate insisted with unexpected solemnity that he must be older than that and put him at thirty-three or thirty-four.

At dinner Gaston and Mama were placed at each end of the table, so that they were facing one another while Renate, Heiner, Fridolin and Lieschen sat on either side of the long table. The table was laid as if for a festive occasion, and the food was good. Mademoiselle Constantine had been asked to eat out that evening.

There was little conversation at table. The old dog, Luxi, lay beside Uncle Gaston, who from time to time absent-mindedly let his fine, rather large hands glide tenderly over the dog's ruffled white coat. The children, with critical and concentrated eyes, kept scrutinising the uncle who was a stranger to them.

After dinner Mama and Uncle Gaston remained sitting on the terrace for a long time. They still didn't talk much; every now and again they said something to each other they found humorous, for they often laughed. They were so deep in thought they did not notice when it became dark. They didn't even switch on the lights when it became no longer possible to make out each other's silhouette. They went on sitting opposite each other.

'Is father bad-tempered?' asked Christiane and laughed quietly. 'I don't see him very often,' replied her brother, 'but when I do see him he usually grumbles and loses his temper.' They did not mention their father after that.

They walked in the garden in the twilight. The white paths stood out in the dark and you could not miss them. Only the black bushes sometimes spilled over onto the paths so that every now and then they would be submerged in the shadows. What could Christiane and Gaston talk about? Would she be asking him about his life in the big cities? Certainly he would have had the same kind of experiences as she, only they were of a different nature and most likely had occurred more than once. There existed between them the same quiet, secretive attachment which exists only between siblings. Each one knew what the other had been through, there was no need for words. They never once mentioned Till, and he never spoke about his suffering. She only asked him about everyday events, and whether he had been successful and what was going on in the theatre world. They referred to little stories connected with their young days and laughed about them.

It was good that he had come.

The heat and closeness which had been so hard to bear were now followed by weeks of serene weather, typical of late summer. Mama's expression changed at last and Uncle Gaston's distant far-away look finally diappeared. Often Mama could be seen walking arm in arm with her handsome brother. Mademoiselle Constantine and Afra commented on the 'distinguished couple'. But as for the origins of Madame, Monsieur Gaston gave nothing away. Was their father, to whom they referred so casually, an old Count or was he a circus clown or a prompter in the theatre where Gaston played the role of the lover?

The children continued to build sand-castles by the river. Mama and their uncle came to watch them and it was the first time for a long while that she spoke kindly and directly to them. 'We are building a palace for Till,' Heiner told them excitedly, 'for him to live in when he comes back — look, there are underground passages and above them ballrooms with marble walls.' Mama bent down low to look inside the underground palace. 'Yes, I can see many passages and ballrooms,' was all she said.

She walked on, holding on to her brother's arm. The air was filled with tranquillity: she was now able to talk about *him*. 'I'm afraid for him' she said quietly, 'his spirit is so volatile and his heart so unruly.'

They paused as they reached the bed planted with asters; Christiane soon got tired when she went for a walk. Her brother looked at the flowers, dark yellow, dark red and white. Christiane leaned on him, she was getting heavier, even standing tired her. 'Will it be a boy?' she suddenly asked and smiled. Her brother did not take his eyes away from the flowers, but only smiled.

VIII

During their walks with Mademoiselle Constantine the children sometimes found themselves in the churchyard. They liked to walk here as much as anywhere else. They didn't pay much attention to where they were, it wasn't very different from other town walks and Mademoiselle was just as bored and stiff wherever it was they went. They read aloud the inscriptions on the gravestones with reverence and some amusement. 'Here lies in peace, Elizabeth Städale, daughter of a landowner,' or 'Here lies in peace, Anton Schallmeyer, the master-baker.' These were all just names to them, sometimes funny, insignificant names, but that didn't really concern them. 'Here lies in peace. . .' was just a way of talking, a little quotation — nothing to do with death. The children had never seen a dead body.

There were two cemeteries, the old one in the middle of the village, near the market, and the other, the new one, further out at the edge of the wood. The children knew that there was 'no more room' in the old cemetery, it had been full for several decades. Here the gravestones were mostly black and worn because the relatives were either dead or had moved away into the town and there was nobody to tend the graves. But the new cemetery was large and at the same time picturesque. Where you read that a child lay 'here in peace', a little girl or a blessed little boy, neat and dainty wreaths made up of forget-me-nots were placed on the gravestones. Sometimes a picture of the deceased was set into the gravestone so you could see what Anton Schallmeyer looked like, with his beard and slim body — or that this is what Lisbeth Munz, stylish and demure, a spinster to the end of her days, was like. On one side of the cemetery a white arcade led to the sanctuary.

One morning when the children were walking in the new cemetery with Mademoiselle Constantine they passed first the gravestones and then continued along under the white arches. It was then that they saw the dead baker's boy. Already from afar they noticed the white construction, the bier, the sheets and the many wreaths. Only at the last moment did they realize there was a young man lying under all those artistically arranged wreaths. They stood still and no one dared say a word, even Mademoiselle Constantine was taken aback.

The waxen hands of the young man were folded across the white sheet. He had a cover over him which came up to his chin but, in addition to that, the lower part of his face, right up to the now pointed nose, had been wrapped around tightly with a white cloth. All that could be seen, under the ugly wreaths and flowers, were his closed eyes, unrelenting and haughty, and his pointed, aristocratic nose.

Mademoiselle Constantine spoke in an unnaturally controlled voice: 'Yes, they have placed him here until he is buried this afternoon.' Renate asked first, her voice hoarse and shaky: 'Who is he — who actually was he?' Mademoiselle Constantine of course knew the answer and was happy to have an excuse to talk. 'He is the baker's assistant, Friedel Muller. He went swimming and drowned the day before yesterday, in the evening. He was bathing in the river after he had had his supper — he had probably eaten too much and that is why he had a stroke. But come along now, children,' she said in a hesitant voice, almost pleading with them, 'why are you standing there?'

The children did not move. All four stared at the bandaged face of the stranger. 'Why have they bandaged up his mouth?' It was Renate who spoke again, and she waited apprehensively for the reply. Mademoiselle Constantine was accommodating and meeker than ever: 'You see — er — the thing is — probably his mouth was open — it must have been open — because he drowned.'

Suddenly Heiner's whole body began to shiver. Of course, that's what it was: he had known it all along, the mouth was open and the white sheets concealed a wailing black mouth. Heiner stared into the face of the baker's assistant. He had never looked at any other face with such intensity. His eyes changed as they stared and became harder — a blue, defiant and brooding hardness. He clenched his teeth so that the muscles in his cheeks stood out, giving his face a more manly look. His whole body shook with fear, yet he stood in front of the corpse with a new, more severe, expression, an expression he would only need to adopt much much later in life.

Renate's eyes rested darkly on the waxen face. Fridolin was apprehensive but interested as if he had been shown a nasty but rare curiosity, a colourful but grotesque-looking object at a fair from which he could not avert his eyes.

Mademoiselle Constantine entreated again: 'Do come along now — you've seen him now.' At last the children took away their eyes from the face that had so absorbed them, and they walked home in silence.

That evening Heiner could not get to sleep for a long time. He was gripped by a fear so terrible, so disturbing, something he had never known before, not a fear of ghosts like you might get on a dark winter's night, a not uncommon fear of little significance. This was the fear of death, or even worse: the terrible unconsolable realization that all of life was destined for death, as were his hands, his face and his body.

When he closed his eyes the face of the baker's assistant appeared before him, but now without the bandages. The black mouth gaping and laughing, wide open with pain, moaned and groaned over his bed. 'Tell me, must I also die one day?' sobbed Heiner addressing the stone cold face. The open mouth, stretching towards eternity answered him: 'It could happen tonight.' Heiner lay on his bed and screamed. Mama sat quietly beside him, stroking his hand to comfort him. 'We could all die any day,' he told Mama, sobbing, 'every one of us — then there might be no people left. . .' Seated heavily on the chair beside him Mama replied: 'But for everyone dead a new person is born.' She bent over her son who was crying and suddenly her eyes were full of tears and she repeated in an even quieter voice, thrilling at the revelation of this secret: 'But for everyone dead a new person is born.'

Next morning Gaston told his sister that he would have to leave the following day.

IX

Shortly after Mama and her handsome brother had left in the horse-drawn carriage the children had the idea of playing the marriage game. It was a long time since they had taken a game so seriously.

They had all four been lying on the grass with very little to say to each other, lazily hoping for something to happen or for some fantastic adventure to shake them out of their apathy, when Heiner suddenly said: 'I would like to marry Renate today.'

Nobody laughed, Renate bowed her head, looking very serious. 'But I haven't yet given my consent,' she said demurely. Heiner smiled at her ingratiatingly: 'Surely you're not going to say no,' he said. 'You have no other suitor.' Renate didn't quite know how to reply to that. 'I think Mama has also just remarried,' Heiner said after a pause, bashful as he bent his head a little lower over the blades of grass he had been playing with. They all nodded, even Lieschen, with a look of incomprehension in her eyes.

The ceremony was to take place in a quarter of an hour and careful preparations were being made. Lieschen was to be bridesmaid and also responsible for the wedding breakfast which was of the highest quality. She managed to obtain some of Afra's dough which she worked carefully, and then laid out little portions onto glass plates. She neatly sliced some apples and placed bread rolls between these. The whole arrangement looked very enticing. There was no other part left for Fridolin but to be the priest. He wrapped himself in his black raincoat looking devious and pious like the wicked Grand Inquisitor. He made himself a clumsy crucifix out of twigs and stood there, barefoot and majestic, on the kitchen chest which was to be the altar, awaiting his prey.

Renate was getting ready. She had decided to put on her white silk Sunday dress without telling Mademoiselle Constantine. Clumsily she pinned a large red aster into her hair. She came down the garden path all dressed up, but she had not remembered to comb her hair: she looked a dishevelled, thin little bride. Her solemn expression and awkward movements showed how unaware she was of her own charm.

Her fiancé, Heiner, ran beaming towards her — his eyes sparkling, but his mouth serious — grandly he offered her his arm. They proceeded slowly towards the 'altar' with the ancient, greying dog Luxi slinking along beside them with great dignity, followed by Lieschen who carried the colourful plates of food in front of her as if they were part of the ritual.

They stood before the 'priest' and looked up at him with a radiant look in their eyes. Wrapped in his sinister-looking coat he held the rickety cross over them as though exorcizing them, and asked: 'Do you really wish to be married? Are you aware that dwarfs will come and destroy you if you are unfaithful to each other; executioners will come to torture you. Will you always and for ever be faithful to each other? For a thousand years? A hundred thousand years? Forever-Pox years?' Their heads bowed, Heiner and Renate replied just audibly 'Yes'.

They were so preoccupied with what they were doing, so involved in the ceremony, they did not notice Mama's arrival. She stood behind them, alone in the bushes, her eyes still wet with tears after saying goodbye to her brother. At first she smiled at the gravity of the children's game, at the priest's absurdly elaborate blessing, at the couple's touching solemnity — but soon her smiles disappeared and her expression became solemn.

It was as though she had never before really seen her children, never seen them so clearly, it almost frightened her. In a second she saw the whole future of her children. Here they were standing side by side promising to be faithful forever. They promised never to leave each other as if they had a foreboding that perhaps one day they would need each other very badly.

Today they were still in high spirits playing games among themselves; today they still believed that they would always be together, be near each other. But life out there was waiting for them, there was no way the four of them could avoid it. Perhaps life was harder than ever, but it was vital they should learn to cope, get the better of it and come to terms with it. Life would overtake them even before they ceased to be children. It would spare them nothing: it would break in upon them with overwhelming gaiety, danger and sorrow. At first they might think that it was just fun and games like everything else. Soon they would realize that life was a serious matter, deadly serious in fact, whether it presented itself with amusement or with pathos.

Their mother knew that they would be steadfast. She knew they would be intrepid, subject to all dangers, involved in every kind of difficulty, but in the end they would cheerfully come through.

What would her children be like in say fifteen years? Christiane could see them all so clearly.

Renate, her head still weighed down by her long hair, shy and withdrawn as ever, self-reliant, cheerful but unapproachable and alone; yet there would be many occasions when in moments of weakness and desire to submit she would be conquered — her dark eyes and beautiful mouth which had become so much softer were proof of that.

Heiner had lost his radiant expression or perhaps it was only hidden by a mask. His forehead was still free of anxiety, though it was shadowed by his lank, unkempt hair. The mouth was his mother's mouth: she could see herself in his careworn youthful face: the same beautiful mouth once so admired by her enraptured husband. But was this softness in her son not open to greater danger? This mouth denied itself nothing nor did it deny anything to others. Beneath his manly forehead was this feminine mouth, abandoning itself without restraint to life. Surely it would soon become old and corrupted if it offered itself to be kissed so ardently. Something in Heiner's behaviour, a tendency to negligence, was disturbing and filled you with foreboding. Nevertheless his mother was not afraid for him.

There was Fridolin, clever, solitary, hard working and extremely ambitious. What did he want? How far did he mean to go? His smug smile was alarming, and he would rub his hands together with an air of self-satisfaction. He turned his unattractive face away from his mother as if he had plans and secrets to hide from her. There was strength in this lonely figure going its own ugly way, climbing difficult paths, pursuing very different objectives from those of his brother, who would say mischievously when he came upon him: 'We know we're related but. . .'

And what about Lieschen? Christiane smiled because she could see clearly what Lieschen was going to be like. To her surprise Lieschen had quickly grown into a mature young lady. It was difficult to say whether she was happy or not. Did she love her husband? Or did she suffer at his side? She never said very much. She accepted her uneventful fate with good humour, while her brothers and sisters went their more adventurous ways. Soon Christiane would be a grandmother; she could already see Lieschen's healthy children playing in the sand.

Never before had she seen her children's future so clearly. How fast they would now develop, each one embracing their desires, facing the dangers and aspirations of life. Should she be anxious on their behalf? At this moment she was so preoccupied by the inevitability of what would happen to them she did not allow herself to worry about them.

She turned away and slowly walked through the garden.

On these late summer afternoons the garden was inert, not a leaf stirred. She went and sat down on her bench, there was no place in the world quieter than here on this bench.

She found this extreme clarity of vision hard to endure. Each leaf was still, simply following the course of its own life. There was no passion, nothing to make things easier or more difficult, no wind to bring disorder or disturbance. Life revealed itself to her at this moment with merciless clarity. It had to be faced for what it was.

The four children she had given birth to were growing up. Four destinies started with her and would complete a cycle. A fifth child was growing inside her. *That is how it is*.

There were not two kinds of life as she had thought the night when she had been so elated. The quiet and the active life. There was only one kind of life — preparing for death.

She had never been able to understand this, nobody had ever been able to understand this. She didn't try to find an explanation and make any sense of it. Her children would be the ones who would fight to come to terms with life, to conquer and discover its secrets. She sat back meekly; she felt this was the way it was.

The children in the meantime had gone to the wedding feast. Lieschen curtseyed and presented the pastry and slices of apple. The priest ate, his face contorted with well-being. But the bridal couple remained locked in an embrace.

X

Winter had arrived. The fir-trees stood dark and frozen in the snow-covered fields. The Klammer-Weiher was frozen over, and again you could toboggan on Afra's heavy sledge across Farmer Zwicker's land.

How were things with Mama? Was she not becoming stranger week by week?

The children noticed how she was growing more and more unwieldy. She was so fat now she could only take short little steps. Was she eating such an excessive amount that it made her swell up and change so drastically? Her countenance was overwrought but also blissful. Her smile was strained, yet at the same time she seemed strangely cheerful. It was impossible to understand her. Often she would stay in her room all day, just sitting, heavy and inactive, by the window, humming little tunes while her eyes glazed over. Her eyes were more beautiful than ever. The children now had more and more the same feelings of tenderness for their disabled mother, which, in the past, they had only admitted at bedtime. It filled them with a vague sense of shame.

Doctor Beerman made an occasional appearance. The children knew him well as he had visited them and listened to their chests on several occasions when they had colds and fevers. With his carefully trimmed, dark moustache he rushed up and down the stairs, laughing as he washed his hands which smelled fresh and masculine. When he bent down to attend to the children the blood would rise in his face and the veins swell up on his forehead. Jokingly and in bad taste the country doctor teased the children in his deep voice: 'I'm certain Mama has a tapeworm.' But the children didn't believe him.

Mademoiselle Constantine treated Mama gently but not without condescension. Over and over again she could be heard saying that any person with self-respect should really not stay on in this house. To the children she behaved with compassionate, almost maudlin concern, though they didn't understand why. 'You poor little creatures' she said mildly contemptuously — and no longer interfered so regularly with their games. Afra, the cook, had also become a little mysterious, she would make odd remarks, and often stood around whispering with Mademoiselle Constantine.

When the children sat together in the playroom at night whispering to each other, they realized that something of importance was going on around them. If only they had known what it was! It made them uneasy and yet they sensed that it must be something beautiful in spite of Mademoiselle Constantine's condescending sympathy and the mystifying comments of the cook.

Then Mama came into the dimly lit room, her heavy body framed in the door and the four pairs of eyes stared darkly back at her. 'What are you talking about?' she asked with that troubled and happy smile she nowadays almost always had on her face. She knew very well what the children were talking about.

One night the noise reached them; the children heard it half in their sleep — they had really been waiting for it for ages. Preparations had quietly gone on for so long, now something had to happen. Was that the bell? Was that a car arriving? They even thought they could hear someone screaming and moaning.

When next morning they entered the dining-room they found a strange, elderly lady in nurse's uniform leisurely drinking coffee. 'There they are, the children,' she said gaily, 'do you already know that you have a new little sister?'

At first the children didn't understand what she meant; they grew quite pale and Fridolin thought that a witch had finally appeared before him. Seeing the children's alarm the elderly lady let out an ugly laugh.

Just then Dr Beerman joined them, hale and hearty and in good humour: 'Well, well, so the stork has been here,' he announced clapping his hands, 'he may have bitten your Mama in the leg, but he brought a fine little sister in return.'

The children huddled together and suddenly Lieschen began to cry quietly. Heiner merely said: 'Does that make us five?' and tried to smile. But that was not what had frightened them. Their shock and inexplicable fear came from something much deeper.

Mademoiselle Constantine was in a bad mood and looked offended. 'Yes, the stork has been here,' she said sullenly. 'Come along and see what he has brought you.' As they all started to walk across to the room Dr Beerman said to her in a muffled voice with a grave and significant look, 'It was a dangerous confinement.'

The children stood inside the door of the bedroom. Mama smiled at them looking so white, lying in her white bed. Dr Beerman laughed gaily: 'Don't be afraid, little ones, go right in.'

Wide-eyed, they went forward, Renate in front, looking suspicious. Mama stretched out her beautiful hand towards them but she was too weak to lift her head. She lay there quite still and resigned as if she would never again have the strength or the will to move or raise herself.

In a cot next to her lay the tiny creature on whose account she had suffered so much. The children bent over and looked attentively at the toothless, miserable little mouth and the minute red, clenched fists. Heiner was the first to stroke cautiously the tense little hands. Fridolin was interested but surly. Lieschen still seemed afraid and quietly retreated.

Renate, however, looked at the little baby with an expression in her eyes no one had ever seen before. Her face bowed over the tiny cot suddenly changed and became softer and more femine as she gazed at the newborn child.

'You'll see,' Dr Beerman joked from the back of the room while he scrubbed his hands: 'No one will care a damn about you now. The little one will be the darling. . .'

But the children did not laugh with him.

A bluish hardness suddenly appeared in Heiner's eyes, a hardness he had shown only once before. This expression of defiance in his eyes was in sharp contrast to the tender, perplexed smile on his lips as he bent over his new sister.

Renate suddenly looked up at the mask of her father hanging white and shiny on black velvet above the bed of the woman who had just given birth. Her father's face was unchanged. His strong, contemplative forehead was as serene as ever; there was not a shadow of reproach in his look. Never before had Renate realized how deeply she loved her father's face.

She turned her eyes towards her mother and for the first

time the eyes of mother and daughter met. For the first time their eyes understood one another.

Mama inclined her head and leaned over the child, smiling wearily, and closed her happy eyes.

Very quietly, as if entrusting the child with her secret, she whispered into the little cot: 'This time I very nearly died.'

The Dove I went to feed
Was made of glass;
She did not wish to live
And did not feed on grass.

I thought she wanted water
I didn't know what to do.
And when I tried to stroke her
I found her wet with tears.

Tears — Snow — Dove — glass

SIBLINGS

A PLAY

Inspired by the Novel
Les Enfants Terribles
by Jean Cocteau

Siblings was first presented in this version at the
Lyric Hammersmith, London, on February 2,
1989, by Michael White Productions.
It was directed by Peter Eyre
with the following cast:

Marietta	Rose Hill
Elisabeth	Suzanna Hamilton
Paul	Simon Cutter
Gerard	Mark Tandy
Agatha	Kitty Aldridge
Michael	Steve Elm

Scenery	Philippe Brandt
Costumes	John Bright
The Song of the Dove	Christopher Littlewood
Lighting	Ben Ormerod

The text presented here is the first English
language version of the play *Geschwister*.

Characters

Elisabeth	Sister
Marietta	Maid
Paul	Brother
Gerard	A Friend
Agatha	A Friend
Michael	An American

Siblings (*Geschwister*) was first performed in German on November 12, 1930 at the *Münchner Kammerspiele* under the direction of Richard Revy with Erika Mann as Elisabeth and Wolfgang Liebeneiner as Paul.

Act One

The children's room. Two single beds, a cupboard, table. On the walls photographs cut out from newspapers are pinned up with drawing pins. At the back a door leads onto the landing; on the right is the bathroom, partly visible to the audience.

It's late afternoon. ELISABETH is seated in front of a small dressing table manicuring her nails. MARIETTA stands looking out of the window.

The play is set in Paris.

MARIETTA   It's been snowing again.

ELISABETH silently goes on manicuring her nails.

There's a man opposite in very funny boots. Sort of a creamy colour: he's up to no good — probably a criminal — a murderer — why on earth are you putting red paint on your nails? What a colour!

ELISABETH   (*holding up her hands*) Too violent, do you think?

MARIETTA   Dear God, they're horrible — like congealed blood. Horrible. The world's full of wicked people. Someone was murdered the other day near my home. You have to be careful, Miss Elisabeth. Oh my God, those bloody fingers. What a colour to choose.

ELISABETH   Is it still snowing?

MARIETTA   The man in the creamy shoes has got a woman with him. I can't see her face — she's got the most enormous fur collar. I wonder what they're up to. You may be sure they're up to no good.

ELISABETH   Did you go down to the café to get the vermouth and sandwiches?

MARIETTA   Well, where is Mr Paul?

ELISABETH   Having his afternoon walk.

MARIETTA   Young people are so lucky, walking and running. Their feet are good and strong. Mine are so painful. God, how they hurt. Would you believe that in my day I had a lovely body? Very thin, I was as flat as a board in front with lovely firm breasts. Oh yes — I used to make my fiancé very angry — he's been gone a long time now. He was getting old and there I was, still with a beautiful firm body. Oh yes, young people have lovely slim bodies. You should see my nephew in Toulon. . .

ELISABETH   (*stretching*) Getting through the day is a bore. What's supposed to be so wonderful about daytime, I'd like to know.

MARIETTA   Yes, he's in Toulon, my nephew. His face is tanned, he's a healthy boy, and if you touched his feet

86

you'd feel the strength in them — like electricity. I'll tell you something, Miss Elisabeth, I'd sell my feet for next to nothing anytime.

ELISABETH   How's your poor sister these days?

MARIETTA   How is she? She's dying. I got a postcard from her. 'Sister, dear' she says, 'I'm dying'. I can't go and stay with her now. Oh, I would have loved to have seen Albert, the young lad. What feet he has.!

ELISABETH   It must be almost seven. Paul should be back soon.

MARIETTA   I often wonder if your Mother's death was, you know, quite natural. Your dear Mother. I mean it all seemed to happen so quickly. Suddenly there she was — dead. All very odd, if you ask me.

ELISABETH   Marietta, really — go on — pop down to the café and get us something for supper.

MARIETTA   I'm off, I'm off.

> *She exits, mumbling. ELISABETH hums to herself and continues with her nails.*
>
> *PAUL comes in. He is dressed casually but his tie is flashy. He has a grey hat and carries elegant gloves. ELISABETH doesn't acknowledge him.*

PAUL   I took a different route today.

ELISABETH   Where did you go?

PAUL   I went down those little side streets beside the

Luxembourg Gardens and then into the Arcade near the Odéon.

ELISABETH   Gosh — how tremendously original.

PAUL   I took the Metro. Just for the ride. Made a nice change. My usual walk's down the Champs Elysées and round to the Madeleine. Sometimes I go up to Montmartre for a little variation. I ate some delicious plums.

ELISABETH   Were they sour?

PAUL   Not at all. They were excellent. I'm an obsessive eater of fruit — cherries, apples. I long for the strawberry season.

ELISABETH   You're going to have a long wait. Like a year. So what else was on your agenda?

PAUL   You should have seen the sky behind the Luxembourg. What other city in the world has sky like ours? Pure silver.

ELISABETH   You don't know any other city, you ass. Did you pick up any new girls — any little conquests?

PAUL   Two children were my entertainment.

ELISABETH   You're a spook.

PAUL   The boy was about 13. The girl 11. The boy was fair, a rather Scandinavian type. He was a bit like Dargelos.

ELISABETH   I knew you were about to start yakking on about Dargelos. Whenever you're in one of your sentimental moods you always manage to drag in his name.

PAUL   He had the same eyes. The icy stare — grey-green eyes which mesmerize you when they fix on you. What else did I do today? Well, I had a nice long steam at the Turkish Baths and then rewarded myself with a visit to a cake shop.

ELISABETH   It sounds like a well spent afternoon.

PAUL   They had the most superb chestnut pastries there — and at the Baths. . .

ELISABETH   That's quite enough of that.

PAUL   Why, my dear idiot?

ELISABETH   I'm not interested in hearing about the children, and I don't find the minute details of your day all that fascinating.

PAUL   (*sincerely*) But I want you to know everything I do.

ELISABETH   My own fantasy life is a lot more rewarding than all this.

PAUL   It was a terrific afternoon.

> *A knock on the door. MARIETTA and GERARD enter. He is clutching glasses and a bottle of vermouth. She is carrying a tray. On it are plates, salt, hard-boiled eggs and sandwiches. MARIETTA puts down the tray.*

GERARD   Good evening, my angels. How are you, Paul? Poor Marietta — she had too much to carry.

> *They place the food on the table, then MARIETTA leaves.*

What do we do first? Eat or arrange The Room?

ELISABETH   You must be joking. Eat, I'm starving. (*She bites into a hard-boiled egg*).

PAUL   (*a glass of vermouth in one hand, a sandwich in the other*) I'm most concerned. You know what? We haven't mentioned the Krox Woman for ages. It's bad luck.

ELISABETH   Shut up, monster. Wait till The Room's arranged. To talk about her during supper would be very wicked.

PAUL   But to talk about the Krox Man — that's permitted.

ELISABETH   I'm sure you realize that in his own special way the Krox Man is as sacred as the Krox Woman. It's true he's more elusive. Of course, she can be very temperamental at times.

PAUL   Now that's blasphemy.

GERARD   Children! Please! Keep very calm. I've brought you — chocolates.

> *He pulls out a crumpled paper bag from his pocket.*

ELISABETH   Melted chocolates warmed up by your sweaty body. Disgusting.

PAUL   I want the cherry brandy.

ELISABETH   That's my favourite.

PAUL   You're too grown-up for the cherry brandy.

ELISABETH   You can have the nut chocolate.

PAUL   I'm not going near that cream disaster.

ELISABETH   Maybe there are two cherry brandies.

PAUL   There's only one I can see — and it's mine, thank you very much.

> *He goes into the bathroom and starts running a bath.*

ELISABETH   Are you having a bath now?

PAUL   Most certainly, my dear cousin.

ELISABETH   You know very well, dear Grandpapa, you had your bath only yesterday. There'll be nothing but freezing cold water left for me.

PAUL   Lukewarm — to be precise.

ELISABETH   I've been asking myself for at least ten years — where are you most likely to end up — a nut house or a prison?

PAUL   Don't be a bore. Come and have a bath with me. (*ELISABETH does not answer*) Krox Woman always bathed in the same bath as her relatives.

ELISABETH   You see, Gerard, how he lies? It's a pathological failing.

GERARD   You're both being extremely obnoxious tonight.

ELISABETH   (*coughing convulsively*) Ugh! He's in there, smoking those American cigarettes. I'm going to cough myself to death.

PAUL   Hold on a minute — I don't want to miss your death.

ELISABETH   I'm serious now. I'm going to pack my bags and move into the Ritz.

PAUL Keep your eyes open, Gerard. Make sure she doesn't nick anything from The Collection. Do you really think your uncle will pay her hotel bill?

ELISABETH I'll sleep with him.

PAUL You should pay him. Don't forget you're as ugly as sin and you're not improving with age.

ELISABETH Ha! You can talk — with your bumpy nose and piggy cheeks.

PAUL Wrinkled old cow!

ELISABETH Right, I'm coming in to get you.

> *She goes into the bathroom. They can be heard splashing each other with bathwater.*

GERARD I'll make myself useful.

> *He sets to work methodically. Places a red scarf over the lamp, switches on the red light by the bed, opens wide the cupboard doors which have been carefully lined with photographs cut out of newspapers. He takes a pile of crumpled dirty linen from the cupboard and sets it in the centre of the room. On top he places a black mammy doll. He then lifts out a small casket which contains The Collection. He opens it and begins to arrange the contents round The Room — several little boxes, artificial flowers, figurines, a revolver, photographs, an imitation snowball, a music box. He winds up the box which plays*

a melancholy tune. While he is arrang-
ing The Room, MARIETTA comes
back to clear up the supper.

MARIETTA   You've taken it all out again, all their rubbish?

GERARD   Yes, Marietta, I have.

MARIETTA   What a funny smell, what is it? They're very
odd, these two. I rather like that smell.

> *She stumps out of the room. ELISA-*
> *BETH and PAUL come out of the*
> *bathroom. Both are in dressing gowns.*

ELISABETH   You shouldn't have put the music on. We're
not in bed yet.

PAUL   The snowball is in the wrong place. It goes
between the revolver and the photograph of Dargelos.

ELISABETH   That's wrong too. The most significant Krox
objet is upside-down.

GERARD   I did my best.

PAUL   The snowball looks extraordinarily real. It's
exactly like the one which hit me on the head. Would
you like to hear the story?

ELISABETH   We all know it backwards.

PAUL   That's no excuse. You might as well say we all
know The Song of the Dove so well it's not worth
singing again.

ELISABETH   (*seriously but mechanically*)

The Dove I went to feed

93

Was made of glass;
She did not wish to live
And did not feed on grass.

PAUL   We were chucking snowballs at each other in the
yard. Why did Dargelos choose me as his target? He
couldn't have known I was always thinking of him.
The snowball hit me, hard, straight at my forehead. It
made me unconscious.

ELISABETH

I thought she wanted water
I didn't know what to do.

PAUL   Gerard, you drove me home. How I cried. Snow
and tears. My face was all swollen, and you, you
monster, you began to shout at me, and then, to calm
me down, you made me play our room game.

ELISABETH

And when I tried to stroke her
I found her wet with tears.

PAUL   We added Dargelos' photo to the collection. The
artificial snowball, of course, had to become part of it
too. Good, kind Gerard. Thank you.

GERARD   What have I done to deserve this?

PAUL   You've always been such a good, loyal friend. And
talented. After all you made the artificial snowball
yourself.

ELISABETH   And you gave us that pretty little revolver.

PAUL   And your kind uncle pays for us.

ELISABETH   Friend to the young!

GERARD   Children, you're teasing me.

PAUL   Let's have some music in honour of your uncle.

> *He winds up the music box. The three are lying on the bed.*

GERARD   Since you're being so spooky, we might as well talk about The Kroxes.

ELISABETH   (*as if reciting a Litany*) Krox — the Great.

PAUL   The all embracing spirit.

ELISABETH   And at her side the very dangerous Krox Man.

PAUL   Oh, to wander once more with the Krox Woman.

ELISABETH   Through the forest of the Seven Nights.

PAUL   Into the valley of grief, all covered in snow.

ELISABETH   A shimmering white valley.

PAUL   Somewhere — the child hurt by the snowball.

ELISABETH   With the bleeding wound on his head.

PAUL   From which he never quite recovers . . . and Dargelos, the huntsman, with his bow and arrow.

ELISABETH   Relentlessly hunting in the snow.

PAUL   Through the valley of grief.

ELISABETH   To the Krox Citadel.

PAUL   Our room extended—

GERARD   (*softly*) Extended how far?

ELISABETH   As far as the eye can see.

PAUL   What have you got under the bed?

ELISABETH   Nothing — of any importance.

PAUL   You're up to something.

ELISABETH   A little light refreshment. (*She lifts up a bowl of crab claws*)

PAUL   Mm. Cherry trifle?

ELISABETH   Crab claws.

PAUL   Horrors!

ELISABETH   Why? You object?

PAUL   Crab — after supper?

ELISABETH   I'm glad it revolts you. I was worried you'd want some.

PAUL   Would anything stop me?

ELISABETH   I've almost had the lot.

PAUL   You're not serious.

ELISABETH   After this one there's only one piece left.

PAUL   You know how passionate I am about them.

ELISABETH   The last one is going straight into my mouth.

PAUL   My hunger pains will give me insomnia.

> *He lies flat, covers himself and closes his eyes.*

ELISABETH   Here — have one little crab claw.

PAUL   I'm going to sleep.

ELISABETH Go on, have it.

PAUL I'm dreaming about a black lady on a bicycle.

ELISABETH Liar. EAT.

> *She puts the crab claw into his mouth.*
> *He spits it into her face.*

ELISABETH (*hurt*) La comedia e finita.

PAUL Sweet dreams for me. (*He turns on his side*)

ELISABETH Can he really fall asleep so easily?

GERARD He certainly can. Sleeping is what he does best. So.

ELISABETH Ah.

GERARD Did he irritate you terribly?

ELISABETH To the point of madness.

> *Carefully and tenderly she covers up the*
> *sleeping figure and smooths his hair.*

What an extraordinary thing — a face. He always seems to have his mouth half open when he's asleep. If you look long enough into a face, it's like studying a landscape. Look at the line from the nose to the lips, and those shadows flitting across his forehead. Everything seems to concentrate on one tiny spot between the eyebrows. I could scrutinize his face for hours. He might have bothered to brush his hair, the naughty boy.

GERARD Does he still have a scar?

ELISABETH From the snowball? He combs his hair

carefully to hide the scar. (*She pulls up a strand of hair*). It's still quite blue. Ugh.

GERARD   He's never completely recovered from it.

ELISABETH   Do you think he's mentally disturbed?

GERARD   Really, Elisabeth. Of course he's not disturbed.

ELISABETH   Remember the time you were invited to stay at that seaside hotel. Paul was always nicking things from the shop — that was definitely pathological.

GERARD   You did the nicking with him.

ELISABETH   Italian books we couldn't read, hideous china figures, useless bits of trivia — maybe I was ill too.

GERARD   Now you're talking nonsense.

ELISABETH   Paul's reaction to our Mother's death was also, God knows, not normal. Neither of us was ever close to Mama.

GERARD   Still she was your Mother.

ELISABETH   First she drove our poor fun-loving Father to his grave, and then after she had a stroke she sat immobile in a chair for five years. It was, of course, most unfortunate that Paul was sitting behind her, chatting away for ages, when he realized the reason why she didn't answer some question was because she had died. He screamed all night after that.

GERARD   To be having a conversation with a dead person is not exactly one of life's great pleasures.

ELISABETH   Is a dead person any more sinister than a live

one? To be dead is after all quite natural. Only life is sinister.

GERARD   Ah. The philosophy hour is upon us.

ELISABETH   You asked about Paul's scar. You see, the snowball somehow transformed him.

GERARD   Are you serious? You're saying a snowball thrown by old Dargelos—

ELISABETH   The snowball was his education. He entered a poetic place of doves and tears. Our room is not lit by ordinary lamps — it's lit by a magical light which comes from the snow world. That's how Paul chooses it to be.

GERARD   Paul may — but can you stand it?

ELISABETH   How could I change my life? Do you think it's possible, Gerard?

GERARD   I'm sure it is.

ELISABETH   For a while — perhaps—

GERARD   You two can't go on like this.

ELISABETH   Maybe you're right. But what am I to do?

GERARD   I've wanted to talk to you for some time. You really mustn't go on like this.

ELISABETH   You've already said that.

GERARD   I know my uncle looks after you and I'm sure he'll continue to do so. That's not a problem. It's your way of life here — it's destroying you.

ELISABETH   And this has only dawned on you now, darling?

GERARD   I didn't want to have to think about it. I'm surprised I can talk to you about it now. You were always — you are for me — beyond all criticism.

ELISABETH   How good of you to say so, dear Professor.

GERARD   I'm trying to be serious. Listen! Lately I've talked a lot about all this with my uncle. As a business man he's very much a man who's involved in the world. He believes passionately everyone no matter who they are should not opt out. You must work, Elisabeth.

ELISABETH   (*as though saying a foreign or unfamiliar word*) Work.

GERARD   I've thought it all through. A young relation of ours — Agatha Dubos, has been working in a big fashion house whose director is a colleague of my uncle's. Agatha is also an orphan — she had a very sad childhood. You might like her, actually.

ELISABETH   What work does your Agatha do in this fashion place?

GERARD   She models dresses. She is a mannequin.

ELISABETH   And you think that might be a specially suitable occupation for me?

GERARD   It's not important what you do, as long as you do something.

ELISABETH   It's true I have a very good body.

GERARD   I worry about you a great deal, Elisabeth.

ELISABETH   It's odd how these conversations with your uncle have changed you.

GERARD   Something else has changed me.

ELISABETH   It must be something very profound judging by your tone of voice.

GERARD   Things have changed, Elisabeth. We're not children any more. I'm thinking about our future.

ELISABETH   Now you're becoming boring.

GERARD   Sorry. I didn't mean to start all that.

ELISABETH   What about Paul? Is he going to be stuck here, a lonely recluse?

GERARD   Paul is ill.

ELISABETH   (*bends over her brother*) He would be horrified at the idea of my earning money as a model. (*Suddenly businesslike*) Gerard, you know I've taken everything in you said.

GERARD   So my prattle has not been entirely in vain?

ELISABETH   No, Gerard. I want to work.

GERARD   (*tries to take her hand to kiss it*) Dear Elisabeth—

ELISABETH   (*pulls away and leans over PAUL*) Will he cry, I wonder? It's a long time since I saw him cry. Do you think he heard all this? No, I don't think he'd manage to control himself for so long. (*She shakes him gently*) Paul, Paul! — I'm going to become a mannequin.

PAUL   Can't you let me sleep, Beast?

ELISABETH   Something rather important has come up —
Paul.

PAUL   I'm not interested.

ELISABETH   Things are going to change now.

PAUL   I've had a weird dream. A detective story, a thriller
— you decided to destroy everything out of sheer
spite.

ELISABETH   Go back to sleep if you're not interested.

PAUL   Now you have woken me, you might as well tell
me.

ELISABETH   No, I don't want to now.

PAUL   You're the foulest creature on God's earth.

ELISABETH   Good. You'll be able to celebrate when you
no longer find me at home tomorrow.

PAUL   Rubbish.

ELISABETH   Things are going to change.

Act Two

PAUL is sitting alone at the table, working with paper and glue. He is silently writing. After a moment AGATHA enters. She is wearing a coat and hat.

AGATHA   Good evening, Paul.

PAUL   (*not looking up*) You're by yourself?

AGATHA   Elisabeth sent me ahead to keep you company.

PAUL   (*still bent over his work*) Is she eating out again tonight?

AGATHA   She'll be back straight after dinner.

Short pause.

What are you making?

PAUL   I spend my day like a ponce.

AGATHA   Is it a dove?

PAUL   Ah — it must be coming together.

AGATHA   And near the eyes — do I see tears?

PAUL   And the threatening object flying towards it — a snowball.

AGATHA   A very strange composition.

PAUL   Dove — Snow — Tears. Don't you spot the connection? (*Pushes the work aside*) It's pointless. I'm fed up with it.

AGATHA   What's the matter?

PAUL   Who is Elisabeth messing around with tonight?

AGATHA   Paul, you know perfectly well she's with that friend of Gerard's uncle.

PAUL   Always with the American. How amusing for her. She has dinner with him every evening.

AGATHA   At seven o'clock on the dot, every evening, he's there waiting for her to finish work.

PAUL   Waiting for a mannequin. FANTASTIC. GREAT. I wonder if he's had her yet?

AGATHA   Paul, I think he has great respect for Elisbeth. I'm sure he loves her deeply.

PAUL   (*laughing*) Love is such a wonderful thing. Love — how absolutely tremendous. As a matter of fact, I couldn't care less what my esteemed sister does. She's a hopeless case. What I do mind is your involvement.

AGATHA   What are you talking about? It's nothing to do with me. Until I met Elisabeth, I led a very dubious life. Elisabeth has had an extraordinary influence on me. She's incorruptible.

PAUL   God, when I think of Elisabeth with her rotten figure parading in the latest creation from the House of Patou in front of some ancient English bitch! Why on earth did Gerard persuade her to become a manne-

quin — where does Mr Michael take her, do you
know?

AGATHA   I have no idea. But I'm sure they're very
acceptable places.

PAUL   So he wants to marry her?

AGATHA   I really don't know, Paul.

PAUL   (*jumps up almost in tears*) Idiot! Idiot! Idiot! The
gentleman from New York wants to get his hands on
Elisabeth.

AGATHA   Why do you put it like that? If he really wants to
marry her 'getting his hands on her' is not a very
precise description.

PAUL   It's just a stupid expression we used as children.
When we were — oh, very young — Elisabeth and I
were told that if we gave each other a kiss or even
touched each other we would immediately go to hell,
like IMMEDIATELY — at that very moment. 'Don't get
your hands on her' — Marietta must have said that,
or some earlier maid from a pre-historic age.

AGATHA   I've noticed how you never kiss each other.

PAUL   Maybe so. If we did we would certainly go straight
to hell. (*He points to all the newspaper cuttings*) How do
you like our picture gallery?

AGATHA   Who are these people?

PAUL   Boxers. Film stars. Murderers.

AGATHA   They all look alike.

PAUL   Do you think?

AGATHA   Look at those cheekbones — and the cruel eyes.

PAUL   You're a bit like them yourself.

AGATHA   Oh come on — hardly.

PAUL   They do have a similar physiognomy — now I think about it. Dargelos' features.

AGATHA   Who was Dargelos?

PAUL   I must have told you about him?

AGATHA   The boy who threw the snowball?

PAUL   Straight at my forehead. He never bothered to visit me when I was ill, even though I was in bed for months.

AGATHA   When did it happen?

PAUL   When we were at school. Dargelos was expelled.

AGATHA   What! Because of a snowball?

PAUL   The old duffers didn't know what really happened. I never told anyone — the snowball was packed round a stone — like cottonwool.

AGATHA   What a monster.

PAUL   It's true. Fantastic! And when he was questioned he threw pepper into the Headmaster's face. He almost blinded the old bastard.

AGATHA   Fantastic!

PAUL   Now you tell me something.

AGATHA   I have nothing interesting to tell.

PAUL   I'll find it interesting.

AGATHA   There are only things I'm ashamed of. You don't know how terrible the world is.

PAUL   It's bad.

AGATHA   There's not much hope.

PAUL   There's a lot of poverty, isn't there?

AGATHA   In my group there were drugs. Do you know when I first met you two I thought you were both shooting drugs?

PAUL   What made you think that? How silly.

AGATHA   Most people out there who don't want to conform inject themselves or swallow something.

PAUL   As if we needed such things.

AGATHA   I soon realized you didn't. This room is too refined for such coarseness.

PAUL   You've adapted very quickly to our world.

AGATHA   I can't remember now what my life was like before. Even though I don't understand a lot of what goes on here. Who on earth is the Krox Woman?

PAUL   Don't ask. She's very powerful.

AGATHA   You must be patient with me.

PAUL   It's odd — I never noticed before how much you look like Dargelos. His hair used to be quite fair, though I expect it became darker with time.

He continues to stare at her.

AGATHA   You're fantasizing, Paul.

PAUL   As if I didn't have a clear memory of his face.

AGATHA   (*relieved as she hears footsteps*) That must be Elisabeth.

> *PAUL turns away as ELISABETH enters with GERARD.*

ELISABETH   Am I disturbing an intimate scene at the hour of twilight?

AGATHA   We've been waiting for you.

GERARD   The master doesn't think us worthy of a glance.

PAUL   (*turning round*) I know everything.

ELISABETH   What, darling?

PAUL   Don't try to do your cool act. I know now who you go out with every evening. I know what you do with your chap. I know. I know it all.

ELISABETH   Actually he's coming here in a minute.

PAUL   You're letting him come here?

ELISABETH   He's just taking a quick spin through the Bois de Boulogne in his racing car.

PAUL   Bloody cheek.

GERARD   Paul, we're talking about an extremely nice — decent person.

PAUL   You can shut up for a start. Who was it that sold my sister? Christ knows what that American shit paid for her. You and your ridiculous American and your stupid uncle — to hell with all of you.

He goes into the bathroom.

ELISABETH   Idiot.

She follows him.

GERARD   Why did he get himself into such a state?

AGATHA   He suffers.

GERARD   What's Michael ever done to him?

AGATHA   I've seen so many people suffer. Seeing my poor Mother was terrible but I learned to bear it, but to watch him suffer is beyond me.

GERARD   Elisabeth is trying to hurt him — on purpose. She flirts with Michael mainly to make Paul angry.

AGATHA   Is Michael worthy of her?

GERARD   He's completely fallen under her spell. Once he was a strong person. Nowadays he has no will of his own.

AGATHA   How strange for an American to be like that.

GERARD   Yet he's never ever been here in The Room.

AGATHA   Then he can have no idea what he's got himself into. I worry about Paul. Will he survive this?

GERARD   When Paul was about 10 or 11 he was sent to some sort of clinic where Elisabeth was not allowed. On the second day of being separated from her, he became so ill the doctors had to send him home. He needs Elisabeth as much as he needs the air to breathe.

AGATHA   Gerard, we must make a solemn promise never

to love any other people except those two.

GERARD   What are you talking about?

AGATHA   That's the way it has to be.

> *BLACKOUT.*

> *The light comes up on the bathroom.
> ELISABETH is sitting on the edge of
> the bath dangling her legs. PAUL is in
> front of the washbasin, energetically
> brushing his teeth.*

ELISABETH   You're even stupider than I thought possible, Paul.

> *PAUL gargles noisily.*

I'm telling you he's a good man. He's really not bad at all.

PAUL   I couldn't care less whether he's bad or not.

ELISABETH   He has a lot going for him — a vast fortune — his racing cars — and his Palace near the Etoile.

PAUL   Great wealth makes me sick — cars — I couldn't give a shit — and I'm not going near his Palace.

ELISABETH   He has a lovely, elegant body.

PAUL   Shut up, you slut.

ELISABETH   After all, I need a little erotic stimulation.

PAUL   (*scrubbing his nails*) I'm not here — I'm not listening any more.

ELISABETH   He's really not bad at all, you know. He

could be one of us one day.

PAUL   Thank God I've gone deaf.

ELISABETH   You see — he comes from the world out there. That's why he sometimes seems a little ridiculous.

PAUL   (*calls to AGATHA*) Agatha, would you please tell my sister to stop talking about some foreign person who is of no interest to me. This conversation is very boring.

ELISABETH   (*unperturbed*) He's already become attached to all of us. He is really very fond of me.

PAUL   Good luck to him.

ELISABETH   Don't worry about him. He can take care of himself.

PAUL   He'll convert you — to his world.

ELISABETH   Idiot. Come and sit down.

> *PAUL sits next to her on the edge of the bath.*

For once in your life try to be reasonable. Must I invoke the Krox Woman to get your full attention?

PAUL   To bring the Krox Woman into this is utter bad taste.

ELISABETH   I sincerely believe this marriage would be right for me. It would also free us from being dependent on Gerard's ludicrous uncle.

PAUL   Why have you suddenly become such a complete businesswoman?

ELISABETH   There would be other advantages. My suitor has potential.

PAUL   For what?

ELISABETH   You'll see for yourself. He should be here soon. Listen. When he arrives, if you think he really won't do say 'Krox Man'. If, on the other hand, you think we should consider him say 'Snowball'. No — that's no good. 'Snowball' would be too conspicuous — if you like him at all just say 'Dead'.

PAUL   It's sweet of you to give me such authority.

ELISABETH   (*angry*) Thank you very much. I'm interested in your opinion because you and I are bound together in everything. I've already made up my mind.

PAUL   What's to become of me when you're the rich bitch?

MARIETTA comes in.

MARIETTA   You have a visitor, Miss Elisabeth. A handsome young gentleman in a lovely overcoat.

ELISABETH   Ask him in, old thing.

MARIETTA   In here? Where are your manners, Miss Elisabeth?

ELISABETH   Go on. Get your skates on.

MARIETTA   (*to herself*) Well, I don't know. It's not right. She's shameless, it's indecent.

> *PAUL and ELISABETH sit motionless on the edge of the bath looking at the door. MICHAEL is shown in by MARI-*

ETTA who stands by the door noisily clearing her throat. He is no longer young but he is in good shape. A clean-cut intelligent-looking American businessman.

MARIETTA   Here's your visitor.

MICHAEL   Good evening, Elisabeth. You're receiving me in the cosiest room in your apartment, I guess. (*Pause*) So this is your kid brother?

PAUL   'Dead'.

MICHAEL   Pardon me?

BLACKOUT

The scene changes to a room in MICHAEL's Palace near the Etoile. ELISABETH is seated in an armchair. MICHAEL stands next to her.

MICHAEL   Somewhere in my heart there must always have been a secret spot which was waiting for you — which always belonged to you. I feel that's why I gave up my life in America, why I came here. Some part of me must have always been searching for you, Elisabeth.

ELISABETH   It is so lovely here.

MICHAEL   Could you feel at home here?

ELISABETH   Paul is adamant about staying in our old apartment.

MICHAEL   I've a wonderful idea, a truly wonderful, great idea, Elisabeth. There's a little room in this house, totally isolated — a mistake on the part of the architect, in fact, right in the well of the staircase. I don't know why but I've always loved this room more than any other room in the Palace. I used to go and sit in there when I was sad — and that has been often the last few years. Lately I've hoped that one day you might be sitting in there with me. This room, you see, could be made into your room — with your Collection — and all your games.

ELISABETH   Should I marry you for the sake of this secret room?

MICHAEL   I have this feeling — this secret room is like that secret spot in my heart. I'm not accustomed to talking like this.

ELISABETH   This room will grow — it will dominate and take over the entire house.

MICHAEL   That's fine by me, Elisabeth.

ELISABETH   Don't tell me I didn't warn you.

MICHAEL   (*tries to embrace her*) You never allow me to touch you.

ELISABETH   Please. Wait a little longer. Nobody has ever been so close to me as you. Only one person will I kiss — and that only at the appointed hour.

MICHAEL   (*letting her go*) Elisabeth.

ELISABETH   (*taking a few steps away from him*) The more you love me, Michael, the sooner it will be fulfilled.

BLACKOUT

Music is heard. An insistent melody

> *like the tune on the music box. The*
> *lights come up. ELISABETH, PAUL,*
> *GERARD and AGATHA are sitting*
> *dressed in black. The table is covered*
> *with a white tablecloth.*

AGATHA   (*holding her head in her hands*) How terrible. The car turned over twice.

ELISABETH   How often do I have to tell you it wasn't so terrible. You almost don't know it happened — it was so quick.

GERARD   Driving at 120 kilometres—

AGATHA   It's a miracle you're alive, Elisabeth. A true miracle of God.

PAUL   (*laughing*) Or of the devil.

ELISABETH   You wouldn't have recognized him. His face was completely mangled.

AGATHA   Please don't go on. I can't bear to think about it.

ELISABETH   No other end would have been so right for him. Sports cars were his passion. Everything else was merely a sickness.

AGATHA   How can you talk like that? About your husband.

ELISABETH   What could be a more beautiful death? At a speed of 120 kilometres.

AGATHA   Without the last rites. Unprepared — the day after your wedding.

PAUL   Exactly 24 hours after your wedding.

ELISABETH   Strange too, how at that exact moment you
decided to move into his house, after always insisting
you would never leave our old apartment.

PAUL   I don't see anything strange about that.

ELISABETH   The oddest thing was how one wheel of the
car went on turning round, all by itself. Imagine, there
above this silent heap of destruction, the car completely smashed, this one wheel went round and
round, getting slower and slower, while he was
already quite dead. What a cliché.

PAUL   I think we should all go to bed now.

ELISABETH   Have you arranged The Room? The one in
the well of the staircase Michael kept for you?

PAUL   Come and see it.

Act Three

> *PAUL and ELISABETH are arranging
> the little room under the stairs of the
> Etoile Palace to become 'Their Room'.
> PAUL is fixing newspaper cuttings to
> the walls with drawing pins. ELISA-
> BETH is standing in front of the casket
> which contains The Collection, quietly
> playing a mouth organ.*

PAUL   (*reading the print at the back of one of the cuttings*)
Stalin's address to the Workers.

ELISABETH   It serves me right not to have played it for so
long — now it's gone rusty with anger.

PAUL   (*still reading*) National Socialist Rally in Nurem-
berg.

ELISABETH   Our collection of canes — neglected; the jam
collection — neglected. You only notice these things
when you move. It's so long since we played any of our
games. How far did Martersteig fly?

PAUL   (*reading*) Unemployment programme in America
— information from the other world. Warnings.

ELISABETH   Idiot. The answer to the question is: Martersteig will go on flying as long as Krox has any breath left — you're always on about 'the other world'. It doesn't exist. You've hung Valentino in the wrong place. He should be under Jack Dempsey.

PAUL   Agatha is right. They all look like Dargelos. I'd like to arrange to have all my meals in here. That dining room makes me vomit. I also want my bed in here.

ELISABETH   Your tidy little bedroom is being rejected?

PAUL   I'm not interested in tidiness. You can carry on squatting in your Louis XVI room.

ELISABETH   Don't you worry. I won't be leaving you alone for long.

PAUL   I've lost my Josephine Baker doll. She should be sitting on the pile of washing. The elusive creature! Elisabeth.

ELISABETH   Leave me in peace. I'm arranging the candles.

PAUL   (*throws the artificial snowball at her*) Catch.

ELISABETH   (*skilfully catches it and examines it*) What would it taste like if one could eat it?

PAUL   Deadly.

ELISABETH   (*looking around approvingly*) It's almost like it was at home, isn't it?

PAUL   (*turns over pages in an exercise book*) The Krox Litany. Section I. 'The Krox Woman is flitting across the roof which begins to sag from sheer terror.'

ELISABETH   By the way, I know why we have horrid

dreams so often and feel unwell. It's because we've not played the going-to-sleep game for such a long time.

PAUL   The one where our beds become sailboats.

ELISABETH   No, the one where the beds rise, at first slowly, then faster.

PAUL   Of course, so we reach the summit together. Then we would have the same dreams.

ELISABETH   But you wouldn't be able to play that anymore. You need to concentrate hard and to work closely in conjunction with me.

PAUL   Why shouldn't I be able to play that game again?

ELISABETH   You don't concentrate.

PAUL   We used to dream the same dreams for weeks on end.

ELISABETH   The great going-to-sleep game has to be played seriously.

PAUL   Dreams about the soft tinkling of bells in the wood, the wood magically lit by artificial lighting.

ELISABETH   The bell which says — 'Never will I see you again'.

PAUL   There's one I remember vividly — there were thousands of blackbirds perching on black snow — of course it was you who had to have dreams of your own. Always so independent.

ELISABETH   It's quite stupid the way you were talking just now about the 'other world'. Who is there of any importance in that other world?

PAUL   Dargelos rules over it.

ELISABETH   Only with our permission.

PAUL   And Agatha lives there too.

ELISABETH   Idiot. Monster. Idiot.

> *She throws the pillows and a book at him. PAUL does nothing.*
>
> *BLACKOUT*
>
> *The room is quite dark. In the middle there's a camp bed, next to it a little table. At the back there's a small library ladder with three steps. AGATHA is lying on the bed, bent over a photograph. ELISABETH sits on the steps. She stands up, watching for a moment, before speaking.*

ELISABETH   You can never sleep in this damned house — it's always either too noisy or too quiet. To hell with it.

AGATHA   (*hiding the photograph*) Elisabeth, you're not asleep either.

ELISABETH   No. But little girls like you need a lot of sleep. What brings you here? Love-sickness?

AGATHA   Stay with me. I'm glad you're here.

ELISABETH   Always come to me when you need me.

AGATHA   Yes, Elisabeth.

ELISABETH   (*stroking AGATHA's hair*) Your eyes are very red. Why didn't you come before and talk to me?

AGATHA   I love him so much.

ELISABETH   So be happy — be happy.

AGATHA   He knows nothing.

ELISABETH   He must have noticed.

AGATHA   He never looks at me — when he does he looks so unfriendly.

ELISABETH   He's shy, you know how timid he is.

AGATHA   He's not timid in other ways.

ELISABETH   Gerard? Have you ever seen him not timid?

AGATHA   Elisabeth, I'm talking about Paul.

ELISABETH   (*turns away from AGATHA*) Paul, yes, of course, I know. I meant to say Paul. I'm getting my words all mixed up.

AGATHA   I worship Paul. Ever since I first met him. Can you ever forgive me?

ELISABETH   What is there for me to forgive?

AGATHA ·   (*clinging to her*) Elisabeth.

ELISABETH   I'm trying to think how I can help you. After all, I do have some influence over him.

AGATHA   You will help me?

ELISABETH   I want to see you both happy. What is it you like so much about Paul?

AGATHA   Everything. Everything. His forehead — his mouth — his voice. I love his forehead. When I was a child I used to dream of someone like him. I invented this imaginary Prince with white, white skin. I called him The Snow Prince.

ELISABETH   Evidently you know Paul was once badly hurt by a snowball. Since then he has been not quite normal. You're hoping perhaps to marry him?

AGATHA   Don't ask me.

ELISABETH   I need to know. What am I going to tell him?

AGATHA   You're going to talk to him?

ELISABETH   Yes — straightaway.

AGATHA   Elisabeth, I'm afraid.

ELISABETH   Put your fate in my hands. I'll take good care of it.

She hugs AGATHA.

AGATHA   I have faith in you.

ELISABETH   I'll tell him that you have always loved him, that you saw him in your dreams, and you thought of him as your Snow Prince.

AGATHA   I was worried you would be angry with me.

ELISABETH   I want very much to see both of you happy.

She lets go of AGATHA.

BLACKOUT.

GERARD is standing in the middle of the room. ELISABETH comes down from the ladder.

ELISABETH   Why are you still hovering about?

GERARD   The house is full of strange noises. I'm restless, too.

ELISABETH   There's nothing one can do about it. Better go to bed.

GERARD   Paul didn't look at all well today. Is he ill?

ELISABETH   Migraine.

GERARD   Maybe I can help him.

ELISABETH   No, he doesn't want to see anybody. He's probably asleep by now. Go to your room. If I need you for anything I'll send for you.

GERARD   Or come yourself? Elisabeth.

ELISABETH   Or come myself.

GERARD   Elisabeth.

ELISABETH   I've got work to do.

GERARD   What work? Don't send me away.

ELISABETH   I've got to arrange things — put everything in order.

GERARD   I need you more than ever.

ELISABETH   Go to your room.

BLACKOUT.

PAUL is sitting at the table. ELISA-BETH comes down from the ladder.

ELISABETH   Tears?

PAUL   Get out of here.

ELISABETH   Thanks. It's just I'm curious to know why you're crying. It's usually for some obscure reason.

PAUL   You're not human. You have no idea.

ELISABETH   You don't have to look at me while you tell me.

PAUL   Leave me in peace.

ELISABETH   You know very well I wouldn't do that for all the money in the world.

PAUL   All right. Come closer.

ELISABETH   (*stands behind him*) Close enough?

PAUL   For some months—

ELISABETH   Go on.

PAUL   Agatha—

ELISABETH   Oh—

PAUL   She looks so like Dargelos.

ELISABETH   So what?

PAUL   I never thought I could love a woman.

ELISABETH   If I remember rightly you used to fall for a new one every other day.

PAUL   That was bullshit.

ELISABETH   This time is serious.

PAUL   She looks so like Dargelos.

ELISABETH   You poor child.

PAUL   I could be happy.

ELISABETH   Poor pet.

PAUL   Stop this nonsense. I was crying because I'm happy.

ELISABETH   Because you're happy?

PAUL   And with pity for you.

ELISABETH   You should pity yourself. Agatha isn't free any more.

PAUL   She is—

ELISABETH   She confessed everything to me. She was crying too, like you, out of happiness.

PAUL   Is it Gerard?

ELISABETH   They're made for each other. They'll make an ideal couple.

PAUL   I wanted to spend my life with her.

ELISABETH   Why? Because she looks like Dargelos?

PAUL   I could never love another face.

ELISABETH   Take heart. She's not such a loss. I know her now — she's second-rate and sentimental.

PAUL   I love her.

ELISABETH   Why are you crying again?

PAUL   I've no idea what's going to happen. I've written her a letter.

ELISABETH   Idiot. Why? When?

PAUL   An express letter. A couple of hours ago.

ELISABETH   Where you declare your love?

PAUL   I never had the courage to tell her to her face. To tell a girl you love her — it sounds stupid — and it's the very first time.

ELISABETH   She'll make fun of you all right.

PAUL   She'll have to give me an answer. At least I'll know where I stand.

ELISABETH   She's probably reading it now — with Gerard.

PAUL   While I wait to hear — there's still hope.

> *BLACKOUT*
>
> *ELISABETH is alone. She is reading a letter by candlelight.*

ELISABETH   'Don't be angry, Agatha. I love you. On my knees I beg you to answer me. I'm suffering so much, Paul'.

> *Carefully she burns the letter in the flame of the candle. GERARD enters out of the darkness.*

ELISABETH   You're still up.

GERARD   I've been waiting for you.

ELISABETH   You could have found yourself a better occupation.

GERARD   It's the main occupation of my life.

ELISABETH   Wake up. You're living in a fantasy world.

GERARD   My love for you isn't some adolescent crush. It's a true — lasting love.

ELISABETH   I won't allow this kind of talk. You know I'll never love anyone after Michael.

GERARD   After Michael? You must be joking.

ELISABETH   Do you wish to offend me? Why do you suppose I married him?

GERARD   I've never thought about it.

ELISABETH   That's because you're blind to everything around you. You haven't even noticed Agatha's love for you.

GERARD   Agatha's love for me?

ELISABETH   Come on. You're not that innocent. Though I can believe you don't realize how deeply in love with you she is.

GERARD   Agatha — she has eyes only for Paul.

ELISABETH   She cries on his shoulder because you choose to ignore her.

GERARD   What should I do?

ELISABETH   You must marry Agatha. Yes. You must.

> *BLACKOUT.*
>
> *AGATHA is crouching. ELISABETH stands next to her.*

AGATHA   What do you want from me? No. No. No. I don't love Gerard.

ELISABETH   You must marry him. After a week you will

love him. He'll indulge all your whims. Listen, Agatha, please — you could be very happy.

AGATHA   I'm only happy when I see Paul.

ELISABETH   Have you no pride? Now you know he has total contempt for you.

AGATHA   You're so cruel, Elisabeth.

ELISABETH   I want you to be happy, that's all. I have no other friend except you. Trust me. Marry Gerard. Get out of this doomed house. Leave me to look after the sick monster. You'll come and visit me every now and then — and I bet you'll tell me how happy you are.

> *AGATHA buries her head in ELISA-BETH's lap, crying quietly.*
>
> *BLACKOUT*
>
> *ELISABETH nervously rubs her hands. She listens, staring into the darkness.*

ELISABETH   It sounds like someone's crying. Agatha? — or is it Gerard? (*She listens*) Paul? It's Paul. I'm coming, Paul.

Act Four

A small sitting-room bin the Palace. A table, some chairs. ELISABETH greets AGATHA and GERARD who have become typically bourgeois in their style of dress.

AGATHA (*kissing ELISABETH*) What a simply beautiful winter's morning it's been, but you haven't been out yet, darling. You were expecting us, I hope? It's our anniversary today.

ELISABETH I know, my angel. How are things with you, Gerard?

GERARD Work, work, nothing but work. Running a factory takes up all my time. In the end you have to see to everything yourself. People do such stupid things. I'm afraid I'm already beginning to neglect my little wife, isn't that so, my love?

AGATHA We usually manage to have the evenings to ourselves.

ELISABETH So you spend most evenings at home?

AGATHA Very often. Sometimes if there's a good concert we go out.

GERARD   Now that Agatha is pregnant—

ELISABETH   You look more beautiful than ever.

AGATHA   If Gerard has the time, he reads aloud to me. Dickens is my favourite.

ELISABETH   (*puts her hands on their shoulders*) You are really happy, you two?

GERARD   (*extracting himself*) But where is Paul?

ELISABETH   God knows. He's probably still in bed, or reclining on a sofa.

AGATHA   The sofa in that Room?

ELISABETH   Any sofa — anywhere.

AGATHA   I'll go and get him.

GERARD   Don't be silly, love. You should take it easy. I'll go.

> *Exits. For a moment the women are silent.*

AGATHA   You were absolutely right — we are happy.

ELISABETH   You owe me a little thank you — that it all turned out like this.

AGATHA   I'm so grateful to you, Elisabeth.

ELISABETH   He thinks the world of you.

AGATHA   I do believe — I really do — he loves me very much.

ELISABETH   And you? Are you beginning to return his love?

AGATHA   I do my best, and sometimes I think I'm about to succeed.

> *GERARD and PAUL enter, followed by MARIETTA.*

GERARD   Paul has been practising a duet with Marietta.

MARIETTA   Oh dear, practise is hardly the word. Mr Paul knows nothing about music.

PAUL   (*looking dishevelled and irritable. He is wearing black pyjamas*) Marietta will soon be 125 years old. For her to tell me I'm unmusical — that really takes the cake, but, to give her her due, she has mastered some of the Krox songs, which as we know require centuries of study. The Song of the Dove is, however, completely beyond her.

MARIETTA   The Master can be very spiteful. Don't you forget — I'm a respectable widow.

PAUL   Lies, all lies. She's never married. Even her nephew is a bastard.

MARIETTA   What accusings. What a thing to say — to talk like that to a poor servant. What accusings.

PAUL   Don't say 'accusings'. There's no such word.

MARIETTA   You're going to pay for this in the next world. It's not right.

> *She exits. AGATHA and GERARD laugh.*

GERARD   You two are still bickering, I see.

PAUL   You find it amusing, do you?

AGATHA   Yes. The old woman is such a character.

PAUL   'Such a character' — what are you talking about?

AGATHA   I don't follow.

PAUL   Oh, I see. I thought for a moment you had mistaken us for a knitting circle — and were making polite chit-chat.

> *A short uncomfortable pause.*

ELISABETH   Do sit down.

> *She offers coffee and biscuits to GER-ARD and AGATHA who nervously accept. PAUL declines.*

AGATHA   Aren't you feeling well?

PAUL   I had a nasty dream.

ELISABETH   Krox Man?

PAUL   Worse.

GERARD   (*after a pause*) Guess who I ran into the day before yesterday?

PAUL   Dargelos.

GERARD   How did you know?

PAUL   There is nobody else.

AGATHA   You mean the boy I'm supposed to resemble? The one who threw the snowball? How amusing.

ELISABETH   Nonsense. Who says you look like him? He has a brutal face.

GERARD   The resemblance is remarkable, actually. He

132

could easily be taken for Agatha's brother. He looked very healthy and tanned. He'd just come back from the Tropics where he works for a car manufacturer — makes good money apparently.

PAUL   Does he look much older?

GERARD   Not at all — exactly the same. He straightaway asked tenderly after you.

PAUL   How kind.

GERARD   He even gave me a present to give you. He told me when you were boys how you both had been obsessively interested in different kinds of poison and had discussed starting a collection. He said to tell you he's still obsessed.

PAUL   (*very quietly*) He was always consistent.

GERARD   I didn't quite catch—

PAUL remains silent.

GERARD   (*takes out a little parcel wrapped in paper*) He got this in India. He said it was an 'evil concoction'. Highly dangerous. (*Puts it on the table*) Who's brave enough?

ELISABETH   I am.

AGATHA   Don't touch it. Please. I know about drugs.

PAUL   I don't think this will be as harmless as your cocaine.

ELISABETH   (*to PAUL*) Don't you want to unwrap it?

All four stare at the wrapped parcel.

AGATHA   Why have we gone silent?

PAUL   You can smell it through the paper.

> *ELISABETH picks up the ball and starts to unwrap it.*

AGATHA   Don't play with it, Elisabeth. It'll bring bad luck.

> *ELISABETH triumphantly holds up a black apple.*

ELISABETH   A black apple.

PAUL   A black snowball —

GERARD   It looks like snakes rolled up into a ball. Ugh — disgusting.

ELISABETH   It smells of snakes. (*To PAUL*) Have it. It's for you.

AGATHA   Please, Paul — don't take it.

PAUL   (*putting it into his pocket*) Into The Collection it goes. Next to the white snowball.

ELISABETH   We must decide where to put it.

PAUL   That's my responsibility.

ELISABETH   Nothing relating to The Collection is your responsibility alone.

PAUL   But everything to do with Dargelos is. Surely I can be responsible for the present he sent me. Anyway, I don't feel well. Leave me alone.

> *He goes.*

AGATHA   You shouldn't have given him that horrible thing.

GERARD   I couldn't just hang on to it.

AGATHA   Elisabeth better be in charge of it.

ELISABETH   I appreciate your concern.

AGATHA   Please, Elisabeth. Go and see if Paul is all right. We'd better be off now anyway.

ELISABETH   Paul doesn't need anything. I'm going to take a little nap.

AGATHA   Do call me if Paul is ill — please.

She makes to leave.

ELISABETH   What makes you think he's going to be ill?

They all go out. MARIETTA comes in and clears the table. PAUL enters.

PAUL   You looking for something to nick?

MARIETTA   I'm nervous.

PAUL   I suppose someone with funny boots gave you a fright?

MARIETTA   I was thinking — Mr Paul is asleep and Miss Elisabeth is most likely to be off resting.

PAUL   Are you referring to my widowed sister?

MARIETTA   And your priceless collection is all over the place.

PAUL   I'm going to send a telegram.

MARIETTA   Always up to some stupid trick—

PAUL   Is there nothing for you to do in the kitchen?

MARIETTA   I'd like a sit-down.

She sits and watches him.

PAUL   (*picks up the receiver*) Hello? Yes, I want to send a telegram — local — this is Champs Elysées 3095 — the subscriber's name is Elisabeth Tuckerman — yes, Madame Tuckerman, that's right. The telegram goes to Madame Agatha Perru, 2007, rue Vaugirard — Express. Will the lady get the message within 20 minutes? You can relay it to her by phone, can't you? But please — it must be to her personally. The message — *I'm dying* — yes, that's right — *dying* — *As you read this* — read — R-Rome — Read — *It is your fault* — Signature: *Paul*. What? It is a joke, of course — it's a joke — a family joke. She'll understand. Read it back to me please. The telegram is going to Madame Agatha. Madame Tuckerman is the subscriber here. Thank you.

> *During the conversation the stage has become darker. Finally only MARI-ETTA can be seen.*

MARIETTA   (*satisfied with what she has seen*) Aha—

> *The room dissolves into The Room as it was at the beginning of Act Three, piles of washing, dimly lit lamps, newspaper cuttings, various objects. PAUL is crouched on the bed, in one hand the white snowball, in the other the black. He juggles with them. Every now and then he bites on the black one. He begins to sing quietly, moving from side to side as he balances the balls.*

136

PAUL

> The dove I went to feed
> Was made of glass;
> She did not wish to live
> And did not feed on grass.

AGATHA   (*outside the room*) Paul — PAUL—

PAUL

> I thought she wanted water
> I didn't know what to do.
> And when I tried to stroke her
> I found her wet with tears.

> *AGATHA and ELISABETH appear at the door.*

AGATHA   Paul — for God's sake — What did you mean by that telegram?

PAUL   Ah — so there you are.

AGATHA   Explain. Say something.

PAUL   It didn't taste bad at all — like stale spicy chocolate.

AGATHA   Oh no — I knew this would happen. (*She cries*)

PAUL   It didn't taste bad at all.

> *AGATHA goes towards ELISABETH who is standing motionless at the door.*

AGATHA   We must do something, Elisabeth. Get a doctor — telephone — run. He's got to have an antidote.

ELISABETH   I'm not leaving you two alone here.

AGATHA   Elisabeth — have you gone mad? Don't you understand? It's a matter of life and death.

ELISABETH   Maybe he doesn't want to live anymore.

AGATHA   (*rushing out*) Something must be done.

ELISABETH   (*coming nearer to PAUL*) Did it really have a strange spicy taste?

PAUL   Of course. That's what I said.

ELISABETH   One can never tell with you. You're such a little liar.

PAUL   Don't talk to me. I only want to hear Agatha's voice now.

ELISABETH   Perhaps it isn't lethal after all.

PAUL   It will have the effect I want it to have. It's beginning — I'm so thirsty.

ELISABETH   We've only got vermouth.

> *She pours out a glass and gives it to him.*

AGATHA   (*entering*) This will stop you getting cold.

> *She is carrying a hot water bottle.*

PAUL   It's too hot as it is.

AGATHA   It will do you good. I'm going to find something to make you vomit.

PAUL   Stay with me.

AGATHA   Paul, what did you mean when you said it was my fault?

PAUL   What a tiny hand you have! If only you had answered my letter.

AGATHA   What letter?

PAUL   My confession.

AGATHA   What confession?

PAUL   Where I confessed my love for you —

AGATHA   I don't know anything about a letter.

PAUL   You never saw the letter? Ah — Elisabeth.

AGATHA   Elisabeth! How can you just stand there?

ELISABETH   Stop this pathetic whining. We have someone ill in here.

AGATHA   Someone is ill — and whose fault is that? Murderer. Murderer.

PAUL   Sh — stay with me, Agatha. Don't leave me.

AGATHA   Paul. Paul — we have been horribly deceived — Elisabeth is not human — Elisabeth the Devil —

PAUL   Confiscated my letter — told endless lies.

AGATHA   Don't die, Paul. I worship you, you know that.

PAUL   Gerard is not your only love?

AGATHA   It's you, only you — I have always — I love only you — for ever.

PAUL   We could have been happy. I'm thirsty.

ELISABETH   There's still some vermouth left in the glass.

AGATHA   (*tries to grab the glass*) Do you want to go on poisoning him?

ELISABETH   Let go, you fool. I suppose you think your great love will stop him dying of thirst.

AGATHA   Don't drink it, Paul — don't drink it. She's evil. Whatever she gives you — will be your death. Don't you see what she's doing?

PAUL   (*looking straight into ELISABETH's eyes*) You are the Devil.

ELISABETH   Look at me carefully. There's nobody else now — just you and me. A criminal monster, right? I'm a monster.

PAUL   Give me the glass.

ELISABETH   (*hands him the glass and he drinks. She turns to AGATHA*) Get out of here.

AGATHA   Paul — don't let her.

ELISABETH   There's nothing more for you to do here.

MARIETTA   (*at the door*) Do you want me, Miss Elisabeth?

ELISABETH   Yes, I do. See Madame Perru out, Marietta. She doesn't seem to know the way.

AGATHA   Don't let her, Paul — tell her you want me to stay.

> *PAUL raises his hand as if to beckon her to stay and then drops it.*

MARIETTA   Come on, Miss Agatha. I've got an umbrella for you downstairs. It's snowing again.

> *AGATHA leaves followed by MARI-*

ETTA. ELISABETH busies herself round the room, humming to herself. She goes to the basket which contains The Collection. She takes out books, photos, dolls, musical instruments and arranges them around The Room.

PAUL   What are you doing, Monster?

ELISABETH   I'm arranging The Collection

PAUL   What a good idea.

ELISABETH   (*holding up the Josephine Baker doll*) Look, I found her.

PAUL   Ah! What's that you got there?

ELISABETH   What do you think, stupid?

PAUL   I'd say — the revolver.

ELISABETH   Exactly.

PAUL   You're coming with me, then?

ELISABETH   Did you think I'd let you travel on your own?

PAUL   I have the feeling you've added something to The Collection which doesn't really belong there.

ELISABETH   The photo of Michael. It belongs there now.

PAUL   How has he won the right to be there?

ELISABETH   By dying. There's no better way.

PAUL   Did you realize this — even before you married him?

ELISABETH   Funnily enough — I think I did — you must eat the whole apple.

PAUL   It's not necessary now. The game has begun. Tears! Snow! Doves!

ELISABETH   (*holding up the revolver*) Isn't it shiny?

PAUL   It was always the finest piece in The Collection. You should wind up the music box.

ELISABETH   Yes, I nearly forgot.

> *She winds it up. We hear the same tune we heard in Act One.*

PAUL   What are you waiting for?

ELISABETH   For you to get ready, my darling. Did you think I'd go first? I want to watch you. Nothing will separate us now.

PAUL   I would have liked to hear the revolver shot.

ELISABETH   It will be your musical finale.

PAUL   What if you cheat on me?

ELISABETH   Paul — do you really think I would let you down?

PAUL   You know it wasn't easy balancing the snowballs — even though they were the same weight.

ELISABETH   I wish I'd seen you.

PAUL   For a moment I thought there was someone else in The Room. Is the music still playing?

ELISABETH   There are a few bars to go.